"Cliff Cain's *Attunement* prophetically comes to the Western world during a time in great need of guidance and (re)engagement with the natural world. Urging a reclamation of attunement to nature, Dr. Cain journeys through the values, virtues, and perspectives on the natural world of these four spiritual guides who inspire listening to nature, attunement to its rhythms, and, above all, a practical invitation to transform our worldviews and lifeways not only for our own self-transformation, but especially for 'our children and our children's children.' A wonderful and practical exercise in interreligious learning!"

—Hans Gustafson

    Professor and Director of the Jay Phillips Center for Interfaith Learning, University of St. Thomas, St. Paul, Minnesota

"This book is a timely examination of humanity's interactions with the natural world. Professor Cain uses the words and actions of these four spiritual leaders to advocate for better stewardship of our natural resources. He reminds us that we are a part of nature, not separate from it, and he encourages us to live more mindfully, consuming what we need, not simply what we want. All of this is told through the lens of religious figures who were, for the most part, ahead of their time in terms of their regard for the natural world. Through them we gain understanding for the need to care for Earth and its human and nonhuman inhabitants. This is an important message for everyone regardless of their religious commitments and practices."

—Irene Unger

    Associate Professor of Biology and Director of Baker Wetlands, Baker University, Baldwin City, Kansas

"Sound spirituality and sound science share a common goal—to expand our perspective on reality and see the big picture. Theologian and environmental scientist Cliff Cain offers a concise but substantial reflection on what some of the world's greatest holy fools and sacred visionaries can say to us today, who live on the edge of environmental catastrophe. In the lives and words of figures ranging from the Christian saint Francis of Assisi to the Buddhist sage Ryōkan, Cain finds wisdom that speaks to both spiritual and scientific aspects of our current crisis and points to possible routes to reconciliation with the planet, our animal brethren, and ourselves."

—Jeffrey L. Richey
Professor of Asian Studies, Berea College, Berea, Kentucky

Attunement

Attunement

Living in Harmony with Nature

Clifford Chalmers Cain

Foreword by Charles Kimball

WIPF & STOCK · Eugene, Oregon

ATTUNEMENT
Living in Harmony with Nature

Wipf & Stock
An Imprint of Wipf and Stock Publishers
199 W. 8th Ave., Suite 3
Eugene, OR 97401

www.wipfandstock.com

PAPERBACK ISBN: 978-1-5326-4101-5
HARDCOVER ISBN: 978-1-5326-4102-2
EBOOK ISBN: 978-1-5326-4103-9

Manufactured in the U.S.A.   MARCH 3, 2020

To all my students I have taught through the years:
You mustered uncommon courage in selecting my classes,
And then you showed gracious kindness in persevering in them.

And to faculty and staff colleagues, at several universities,
who have enriched my life: Your friendship and support
have meant more than you could ever imagine.

Contents

PERMISSIONS

FOREWORD

CLIFFORD CHALMERS CAIN'S LATEST and timely book is a non-fiction gem. Writing in a compelling, yet accessible, style, he persuasively presents a framework for how human beings can and must relate to the whole of creation. While the importance of his central focus clearly stands the test of time, it is especially relevant in the first quarter of the twenty-first century. Cain has achieved something rare in nonfiction. He has provided a crossover book that can and should be discussed, debated, and utilized by a wide variety of audiences. Why is this book so important, timely, and useful?

The attitudes and actions of humans toward the rest of creation have always been a weighty theological and practical issue. Readily visible examples abound in the major and numerous indigenous religious traditions. Laws governing the Sabbath in the Hebrew Bible, for example, focus on rest and renewal not only for the people of Israel, but also for animals and for the land. Fundamental worldviews in various forms of the Hindu traditions posit the one ultimate reality that binds all creation together. Many indigenous traditions affirm humans as inextricably connected with the world we inhabit. I often begin my course on comparative religion at the University of Oklahoma with a wonderfully insightful and thought-provoking chapter from Barre Toelken's book, *Seeing with a Native Eye*. The author reports on the holistic ways the Navajo view their place in the world. They value and care for the land and water. And, even when taking of life—as in a deer hunt—they are guided by respect for the animal, including humane killing as the hunter apologizes to the animal for taking its life in order to provide essentials for his family and tribe.

The deep theological roots of an inclusive ecological worldview are highlighted throughout the chapters of this book. Cain identifies ways so many in the West have lost or distorted appropriate human respect for and relationships with creation. In addition to a spiritually or theologically based worldview that can inform human behavior, very real and pressing pragmatic issues must now concern everyone. Domination, exploitation, and abuse of the planet for short-term gains is not only selfish, it is self-destructive. Biologists estimate that between one hundred to two hundred species of plants, insects, birds, and mammals become extinct every single day. This may be as high as one thousand times the natural rate. It is certainly dramatically faster than any other time since dinosaurs were decimated sixty-five million years ago. While all of the medium and long-term consequences of this biodiversity loss are not precisely known, the fact that more than 190 nations have signed the Convention on Biological Diversity, a product of the Earth Summit in Rio de Janeiro in 1992, underscores the global consensus.

For several decades, scientific evidence has left no doubt about the human behaviors fueling progressively precipitous changes to the climate. Massive use of fossil fuels and deforestation in South America, Indonesia, and elsewhere are among the most obvious contributors to melting polar caps and increasingly destructive weather systems. Conservatively, 95 to 98 percent of scientists who study and track climate-related data are emphatic: Human behaviors are a major contributor to the ever-faster pace of climate change; the potential consequences in the coming decades are many and dire. And yet, there are many political and business leaders—most notably people with vested interests in lucrative products that are major contributors to degrading the climate we all depend upon—who continue to insist that "scientists are not agreed" or the "jury is still out" on human causes of the changing climate. Jane Mayer's superb study, *Dark Money*, devotes considerable time to tracing how titans in the fossil fuel industries have been effective at changing the narrative from 95 to 98 percent of scientists agree to "scientists disagree" on human contributions to climate change. Mayer traces how major sources of funding impact political candidates and demonstrable changes easing, or eliminating safeguards put in place through the Environmental Protection Agency.

Caught up in short-term benefits, it appears many Americans (and others) can be easily distracted from the serious and possibly irreversible consequences of failing to address the proverbial elephant in the room. Consider the following analogy: Imagine you or your daughter has recurring and deeply troubling medical symptoms requiring the expertise of highly qualified physicians. You go to a doctor who determines the cause is a life-threatening condition requiring surgery without much delay. You then seek a second opinion and get the same diagnosis. Not quite satisfied, you go to a third doctor for more tests and analysis. After visiting one hundred different doctors, you find that ninety-five to ninety-eight of them are in agreement about the nature of the malady and need for immediate surgical intervention. Who among us—assuming we had the means and/or insurance coverage for the life-saving surgery—would respond by saying: "Well, the doctors are not sure," or "The jury is still out on whether or not surgery is needed"?

The world today is vastly different from previous eras. We live in an increasingly interconnected and interdependent world community where the attitudes and actions of human beings toward the rest of creation have global consequences. The environmental challenges we face are not limited by national boundaries; they are challenges for all who inhabit the planet. The 2016 Paris Agreement—an agreement within the United Nations Framework Convention on Climate Change (UNFCCC)—brought all countries into a common cause of combatting climate change and adapting to its effects. In 2017, much to the dismay of leaders around the world, President Donald Trump withdrew the United States as a signatory to the Paris Agreement. Through executive orders and Environmental Protection Agency actions lowering standards for scores of regulations, the Trump administration has eroded safeguards implemented to protect our land, air, and water supplies.

Cliff Cain is ideally qualified to engage both the theological and practical issues converging around human attitudes and actions in relation to the environment. He's a seasoned religious studies teacher-scholar with longstanding interests in and multiple publications about human custodianship of nature. Using the exemplary lives and experiences of four prominent religious figures from different centuries, Cain educates, illuminates, and invites the reader into a perennial conversation that has never been more important. Three of the four people are European Christians; one is an Asian Buddhist. While two figures are very well-known—Saint Francis of Assisi and current Pope Francis—two others—Taigu Ryōkan and Hildegard of Bingen—will be less familiar to many readers.

All readers, I suspect, will be surprised and intrigued as I was by details woven into the narratives of all four figures. A few examples illustrate the point: In the informative chapter on the much beloved Saint Francis of Assisi, Cain creatively connects Francis's worldview and lifestyle with contemporary dangers of rampant consumerism and avarice that reinforce an "I/it" relationship to the world. Building on the well-known "Canticle to Brother Sun and Sister Moon," Cain develops a compelling case for a theocentric rather than anthropocentric worldview, the latter of which readily leads to the desacralization of nature and increased human ecological degradation.

In the chapter on Taigu Ryōkan, Cain gently educates the reader about key elements of Confucian, Daoist, and Buddhist worldviews as he tells the story of this legendary Japanese Buddhist monk. Born in 1758 AD, Ryōkan's poetry captures both his teachings and exemplary lifestyle enveloped in the natural world. His story is appealing as it also reflects cross-cultural wisdom of living in the present and avoiding the trap that "things" do not and cannot bring lasting meaning and happiness in this life. Cain explicates classic Buddhist understandings of impermanence even as he identifies striking parallels to teachings of Jesus echoed in Ryōkan's poetry.

Hildegard of Bingen, the sibyl of the Rhine, is an especially intriguing figure. A woman who was believed to receive and convey messages from God, Hildegard was irrepressible as she challenged the limitations on women who were religious in the male-dominated culture of the twelfth century. A pioneering figure in science, medicine, and music, Hildegard had much to say about human relationships with God's creation—including language about God's lordship and motherhood.

The final major chapter focuses on Pope Francis. Cain presents compelling evidence that the first pope from the Americas is the pontiff to the poor and for nature. Reading Pope Francis's richly documented writings and addresses is both captivating and persuasive. The world's most visible Christian leader's cry for awareness resonates like a fire alarm in the night. Impending ecological crises and their most immediate impact on the poor and marginalized demand urgent action by people of faith and goodwill. Cain not only presents the pontiff's heartfelt admonitions, he deftly shows how Pope Francis is continuing in the traditions of his most recent predecessors—Pope Paul VI, Pope John Paul II, and Pope Benedict XVI.

The concluding chapter fittingly brings the central themes of the book into sharp focus, making clear that a healthy religious worldview can and must facilitate the transformations needed if we hope to live long into a sustainable future on the only planet we have.

The subject matter and accessible writing style will appeal to several target audiences. This is a wonderful book for various undergraduate religious studies classes—from introductory classes and comparative religion to courses on church history and religion and the environment. Similarly, it will be a valuable resource for seminary and divinity school students. It is an ideal resource for thoughtful adult study classes in churches throughout North America. I believe many book clubs will find Cain's text an enjoyable read that is certain to stimulate lively discussion extending beyond the theological and practical foci noted above. In short, as various audiences learn and reflect on human interaction with the environment, they will also be rewarded by discovering thought-provoking nuggets lodged in each chapter of this fine book.

CHARLES KIMBALL

Presidential Professor and Chair
Religious Studies Department
The University of Oklahoma

ACKNOWLEDGMENTS

Special thanks are given to the following persons:

Mr. Jim Tedrick and Mr. Matt Wimer of Cascade Books, for their guidance and patience;

Dr. Charles Kimball, Presidential Professor and Chair of the Religious Studies Department at the University of Oklahoma in Norman, Oklahoma, for the foreword;

Dr. Hans Gustafson, Director of the Jay Phillips Center for Interfaith Learning and Professor in the College of Arts and Sciences at the University of St. Thomas in St. Paul, Minnesota;

Dr. Irene Unger, Associate Professor of Biology and Director of Baker Wetlands at Baker University in Baldwin City, Kansas;

Dr. Jeffrey L. Richey, Professor of Asian Studies at Berea College in Berea, Kentucky;

Ms. Laura J. Wiltshire, Westminster College Class of 2016, for the beautiful photograph, "Mammoth Beauty," on the book's cover.

INTRODUCTION

THE LATE THOMAS BERRY wrote of the importance of "attunement" in living with the natural world, that is, of existing in such a way that one's perspective, values, and actions are in line with the rhythms and cycles of nature. Living in this way means listening to the natural world and allowing its wisdom to inform our actions as humans.[1]

Native Americans and other aboriginal peoples informed and directed their lives by living in tune with the natural world. Indeed, their survival depended upon it. Consequently, the hunter-and-gatherer attitude toward nature was one of knowledge and respect, and behavior was consonant with this attitude. Living in harmony became the communal and individual goal. To do so was to live, even thrive. To not do so was to die.

We have lost this sense of "attunement" today: We see nature as something totally distinct and separate from us humans. The natural world is "out there," a place to which we may go or retreat or journey. We don't think of nature "in here," that we are an inextricable part of what Native Americans and others have called the web of life. From their perspective, we did not weave the web; rather, we are merely a strand in it. We are a part of it; it is a part of us.

---

1. Berry, *Dream of Earth.*

Beyond this, we have then demoted nature to the status of an object. Nature is a vast storehouse of resources—its sole purpose for existence is to supply what we humans want. Its value is to satisfy human beings. Nature is there "for us." So, we can feel confident taking whatever we desire.

Religion, of course, has sometimes endorsed, or has been appealed to in order to sanction, this vision of nature's role. In the example of Western religions, God made the world, but God made the world *for us*. God's mandate is to dominate and subdue (Gen 1), and this apparently gives us the right to do whatever we want to do. Therefore, nature is a commodity to be used; it is not a community with which to relate.

What has resulted is what Berry calls "cultural autism."[2] We live in a way that is separate from (the rest of) the natural world, and we don't listen to it. Oblivious to nature's voice and estranged from nature's touch—somehow believing that we are exempt from nature's laws and nature's power—we manipulate and plunder, despoil and destroy.

Clearly, we have to find our way back—back to our "natural" place in the order of things. To do so is to live, even thrive; to not do so is to die (and to leave an ecological inheritance to our descendants of which we would not be proud and for which they would not be grateful).

We may be aided in our return by the thoughts and lives of four key persons from European and Asian contexts—Hildegard of Bingen from Germany, Francis of Assisi from Italy, Taigu Ryōkan from Japan, and Pope Francis from the Vatican.

But why, especially, should there be yet another book that deals, in part, with Francis of Assisi? From Thomas of Celano to Saint Bonaventure, G. K. Chesterton to Lawrence Cunningham, Nikos Kazantzakis to Paul Sabatier and Leonardo Boff, countless treatments of the most popular saint in Catholicism and the most widely known in all of Christendom have been proffered. These books have described and made relevant the particulars—both historical and legendary—of a life that is worthy of emulation.

2. Berry, *Great Work*, esp. x–xi, 4, 18, 44, 46, 58, 81–82, 115.

From his call to vocation in St. Damiano's Church to the renunciation of his patrimony; from his marriage to Lady Poverty to the founding of a new order; from his visit to Sultan Al-Kamil to his receiving the stigmata to his death at the age of forty-four; and to his canonization two years after that death: these treatments have powerfully presented a unique and inspiring life.

But what is lacking is an in-depth investigation of his life by a theologian who is also an environmental scientist, who applies theological and scientific "green lenses" to flesh out the ecological implications of a life that also called fire a "brother," the moon a "sister," the earth our "mother," the sun a "brother," and animals fellow creatures, sentient subjects, and family members. This project intends this, along with doing the same unprecedented work in regard to several other historical figures—Saint Hildegard of Bingen, the most influential woman of the twelfth century and arguably one of the most influential persons of that century regardless of gender; the eighteenth- and nineteenth-century Japanese Zen monk, Ryōkan, who is a household name in his native country and representative of some of Asian culture's attitudes and actions toward the natural world; and the current pope, Francis, who has powerfully impacted the twenty-first century because of his humility and modesty, his identification with the poor, his simple lifestyle, and his commitment to environmental issues, prominently among them climate change.

How we choose to relate to the natural world of which we are a part and which sustains us is crucial for the future decades of the present century. The degradation, deterioration, and destruction of the web of life which enables our survival as a species will either continue unabated, making planet Earth a very inhospitable place to and for life, or they will be addressed energetically and with decisive action in a spirit of urgency. Nothing short of the survival of the planet—and consequently the survival of all plant (*flora*) and animal (*fauna*) species, including *Homo sapiens*—is at stake.

What will we say to our children, our children's children, and their children, if the relentless ravaging of what Pope Francis calls our "common home" causes the collapse of nature (the "end of nature," as environmentalist Bill McKibben has rightly warned) and therefore destroys the quality of life on Earth or life *per se* on Earth?[3]

What follows, then, is an examination of the values and virtues which describe these four lives and their perspectives on the natural world, on "creation" for three of them and "nature" for the fourth. The insights that we gain may have the power to inform and transform *our* perspectives, *our* lives, and *our* actions. The fate of the natural world hangs in the balance . . . our fate . . . and the fate of our children and our children's children.

CLIFFORD CHALMERS CAIN

Fulton, Missouri
Fall 2019

3. McKibben, *End of Nature.*

Chapter One

HILDEGARD OF BINGEN

The Sibyl of the Rhine[1]

IT IS NOT BREAKING news that the contemporary situation for women in the United States is not equal to that of men. It has improved, but there is not parity. A woman still earns 80.5 cents for every dollar a man earns, and women's median annual earnings are nearly $11,000 less than men's. Beyond this, there are comparatively few women who serve as CEOs of major companies, businesses, and corporations. Over half a century after the passage of the Equal Pay Act, American women still face a substantial gender wage gap across the spectrum. While progress has been made toward pay equivalency between the sexes, the Institute for Women's Policy Research estimates that it will not be reached until 2059.[2]

In terms of voting rights, while the United States declared its independence on July 4, 1776, it was not until August 26, 1920 that the Nineteenth Amendment to the Constitution was enacted and women received the right to vote. Several women in those interim days were "ahead of their time"—Elizabeth Cady Stanton, Susan

1. A sibyl is a woman from ancient times who was believed to utter oracles (messages) and prophecies from a god/God. The earliest sibyls prophesied at holy sites, with the prophecies believed to be influenced by divine inspiration.

2. Sheth et al., "7 Charts," para. 5.

B. Anthony, Jeannette Rankin, Dorothy Day, Sojourner Truth, Ida B. Wells, Alice Paul, and Amelia Bloomer. It was not uncommon for women to be jailed, and sometimes beaten and even tortured, for asking for, and then subsequently demanding, this right of citizenship.

Imagine the situation for women in Europe in the twelfth century of the Middle Ages: "The culture of the twelfth century was a very masculine one,"[3] for "the Middle Ages were resolutely male."[4] Practically speaking, when a woman was born she was formally and legally the property of her father. She was expected to be subservient to him and to other males in the household if she had brothers: "Women were obliged to submit to the decisions of the men of the family."[5] Upon marriage, she became the official and legal property of her husband. She was expected to be "utterly submissive" to him in accordance with sacred Scripture.[6]

> Wives, submit yourselves to your own husbands as you do to the Lord. For the husband is the head of the wife as Christ is the head of the Church, his body, of which he is the Savior. Now as the Church submits to Christ, so also wives should submit to their husbands in everything.[7]

As a result, a woman was under the formal and legal direction of men for her entire life.[8]

Two key, religiously-sanctioned "vocations" were available to a woman at this time: She could wear the wedding veil and get married, or she could "take the veil" and become a nun.[9] Although the second option, living separated from society and cut-off from family and friends, may seem less desirable to us today, the nunnery

---

3. Kettle, Review of *Women of the Twelfth Century*, para. 7.

4. Kettle, Review of *Women of the Twelfth Century*, para. 2.

5. Duby, *Remembering the Dead*, 127.

6. Rosenwein, *Short History*, 239.

7. Eph 5:22–24.

8. Apse, "Medieval Women."

9. Bovey, "Women in Medieval Society," para. 8. Of course, some women would choose to become prostitutes, for a variety of reasons. It was another option, though not one approved by society or the church.

offered freedom from the dangers of child-bearing—20 percent of women in that time died in childbirth; it was 30 percent and higher among the lower class[10]—and gave women the opportunity to obtain an education. As we shall see, a woman—such as Hildegard of Bingen—rising up through the ranks of nuns to become an *abbess*[11] of a convent or a nunnery provided a strong challenge to the stereotypical image of medieval women as oppressed and subservient.

Be that as it may, the clerics of the church, too, were "trapped in their male prejudices and obligated to keep away from women and fear them."[12] As a result, and for example, Pope Innocent III proclaimed in 1210 that Christ gave the keys to the kingdom of heaven to the apostles and not to the Virgin Mary, however exalted her unique status as the "Mother of God" might make her. For Mary was viewed paradoxically as both the human, female conduit for the incarnation of God in Jesus into the flesh of the physical world, *and* the blessed, holy Virgin who had not experienced passion and intercourse and has been venerated as such.

In writing about the exchange of letters between Heloise and Abelard (two former lovers who were now a nun and a monk, respectively), medievalist Betty Radice notes that since women were viewed to be easily seduced by evil and inferior pleasures, such as the enjoyment of sex, Heloise's natural, sexual lust indicates her weaker nature as a woman.[13] While the early church fathers had regarded men as "evil merely from the waist down," women were "rotten from head to toe."[14] And so, in the manuals of "courtly love" (the love of a knight for his lady, perhaps a married noblewoman, regarded as an ennobling passion but not typically involving consummation), males were in control: "As always men . . .

---

10. Trueman, "Medieval Women."

11. The head of a community of nuns; Hildegard technically became a *magistra* or "mistress" rather than an abbess.

12. Duby, *Eve and the Church*, 2.

13. Radice, *Abelard and Heloise*, 82.

14. Dronke, *Women Writers of the Middle Ages*, quoted in Maddocks, *Hildegard of Bingen*, 59.

were the ones who mattered. Women were a race apart, a different and hostile species and a constant source of temptation to men. It was necessary to master them, keep them in seclusion and protect them from their own natures."[15]

With the power of the church pressing downward upon them and the veneration of the Bible bubbling upward from beneath them, women in medieval society had their place often dictated by scriptural texts and church rules: For example, and based on holy Scripture, women were forbidden to teach ("Women shall not instruct men"—1 Tim 2:12a) or to speak ("Women must keep silent"—1 Cor 14:34; 1 Tim 2:12b). Women could not practice medicine, although they could serve as midwives. Women could not be "apothecaries" (pharmacists; druggists) but could be "herbalists" (although not without risk, as this led in some time periods to accusations of witchcraft). Women could not hold political office, like a mayor, or become a judge. Women could not become painters, but could serve as illustrators; so, a woman like Herrad of Landsberg "illustrated" biblical texts and other sacred materials.

In short, in the twelfth century, "women were primarily objects to be used by men who controlled their space and their time."[16] Into this *milieu*, into this historical context, Hildegard of Bingen was born. She would turn out to be a person of her time and also ahead of her time.

Hildegard was born in Bermersheim, Germany, twelve miles southwest of Mainz, in the summer of 1098.[17] Her parents—Hildebert and Mechthilde—according to Godfrey, Hildegard's first biographer, were "wealthy [members of the gentry] and engaged in worldly affairs."[18] They chose to dedicate their daughter to the service of God.[19] According to Guibert of Gembloux (an associate who wrote an uncompleted life of Hildegard), Hildegard was dedicated as a "tithe," and promised to the church since she was the

15. Kettle, Review of *Women in the Twelfth Century*, para. 11.
16. Kettle, Review of *Women of the Twelfth Century*, para. 8.
17. Flanagan, *Visionary Life*, 1.
18. Flanagan, *Visionary Life*, 22.
19. Flanagan, *Visionary Life*, 1.

tenth and last child.[20] The technical term for this is "oblation," the rearing of children destined for a religious life in the cloister, and a number of families did this, though this was traditional but by no means an obligation concerning the tenth child. In fact, some families with only two or three children did it as well. Specifically, this was common among well-born, pious families.[21] So, in 1106, at the age of eight, Hildegard entered the convent, the Cloister at Disibodenberg, "given by her parents as a gift to God."[22] Hildegard says herself, "In my eighth year, I was offered to God for the spiritual life."[23]

Sickly from the time of her birth and of rather fragile health throughout her life,[24] Hildegard lived with "Jutta" and "little Jutta," training for eight years before taking her vows at the age of fourteen on All Saints' Day, November 1, 1112.[25] Jutta was an anchoress, not a nun in a convent of women, so she was required to stay in her cell, completely isolated and closed-off from others and from the outside world until death, and with no hope of ever leaving it.[26] In fact, in the tradition and liturgy of the church, the enclosure of anchorites was liturgically treated as a "burial." Jutta was a rigorous, vigorous ascetic, and wore out her body by her austerities and died on December 22, 1136, at the age of forty-four. By contrast, Hildegard found cogent the Benedictine virtue of moderation—the means between the two extremes of severe asceticism and self-indulgence—and would live to be eighty-one.[27] For example, although fasting could sometimes be overdone in monasteries (after all, the early church fathers had diagnosed Adam's sin not as pride but as gluttony), Hildegard avoided both the excesses of

20. Flanagan, *Visionary Life*, 23.

21. Maddocks, *Woman of Her Age*, 18.

22. Flanagan, *Visionary Life*, 23.

23. Migne, *Patrologia Latina*, vol. 2; quoted in Flanagan, *Hildegard of Bingen*, 16. For more information, see Migne, "Saint Hildegard of Bingen."

24. Newman, "Introduction," 7.

25. Maddocks, *Woman of Her Age*, 22.

26. Flanagan, *Visionary Life*, 29.

27. Newman, "Introduction," 7.

feasting and fasting. "In contrast to Jutta, Hildegard's attitude to food was healthy in its moderation, springing largely from common-sense notions of balance."[28]

Despite such differences between the two women, Jutta had a profound influence on Hildegard: She taught Hildegard the Psalms and showed her how to play the ten-stringed psaltery.[29] Since the psalter (collection of the Psalms) was the "universal primer of the Middle Ages,"[30] this meant that she was taught by Jutta to *read* at an elementary level, though, admittedly, she was no scholar. It also meant that music formed a part of her early education. This would be formative, as she would mature and eventually compose seventy to eighty musical pieces. She learned from Jutta the basics of the religious and moral life and the tenets or rudiments of the Christian faith. She had not been the recipient of any education in her home before entering the abbey, so this meant that she did not have the opportunity to attend a cathedral school, unlike boys of her vocation and status.[31] Therefore, she did *not* go through the seven liberal arts (the *trivium* of grammar, dialectic, and rhetoric, and the *quadrivium* of arithmetic, geometry, astronomy, and music), which was the basis of all education for the learned classes in the Middle Ages.[32] As a result, Hildegard often referred to herself as unlearned (*indocta*), ignorant, simple, and a mere vessel of God. She was obviously and unjustifiably self-effacing in this, but she, indeed, was not trained in the basic education of the upper echelons of the medieval period. At the same time, the humility and modesty she displayed would grant greater credibility and authority to the visions that came to her. In fact, scholar Barbara Newman thinks that Hildegard's lifelong protestations of ignorance should be "taken with no more than a grain of salt."[33] For the main point of her self-deprecation was to emphasize that the source of

28. Maddocks, *Woman of Her Age*, 43.

29. Godefridus and Theodoric, *Vita* 1.1; Maddocks, *Woman of Her Age*, 31.

30. Flanagan, *Visionary Life*, 31.

31. Newman, "Introduction," 6.

32. Newman, "Introduction," 40.

33. Newman, "Introduction," 6.

her revelatory visions was divine, not human.[34] As she would claim regarding them, "These words do not come from a human being, but from the Living Light."[35]

Visions gave women a voice in church and society, because the administration of the sacraments, preaching, and other aspects of the religious life were shut off from them.[36] Women were to be silent and submissive. To be otherwise—vocal and assertive—would have been to prompt the charge of "Eve," for in the medieval Christian mindset it was the boldness of Eve that brought down the fall of humanity.[37] But the receiving and sharing of visions could circumvent these obstructions.

And receive such visions, she *did*. From the age of three, these visions, these revelations, came to her: "I was only in my third year when I saw a heavenly Light which made my soul tremble, but because I was a child I could not speak out."[38] "[This] . . . immense Light . . . shook my soul."[39] She chose not to record these visions because—

> I saw all this and then—I refused to write. Not out of stubbornness, but out of a sense of my inability, for fear of the skepticism of others, the shrugging of shoulders, and the manifold gossip of mankind, until God's scourge threw me on the bed of illness. Therefore, finally, overcome by much suffering, I set my hand to write.[40]

Her visions, then, were not dreams or phenomena induced by fasting or hysteria into a state of ecstasy or trance. Rather, they came to her while she was fully awake and conscious.

However, though "Hildegard may have been fully conscious when she had her visions . . . she seems to have fallen into some

34. Newman, "Introduction," 7.

35. Baird and Ehrman, *Letters of Hildegard*, 1:127.

36. Maddocks, *Woman of Her Age*, 57.

37. Maddocks, *Woman of Her Age*, 59.

38. Godefridus and Theodoric, *Vita* 2.2.

39. Quoted in Maddocks, *Woman of Her Age*, 54.

40. Hildegard, *Hildegard of Bingen*, 59–61.

sort of cataleptic trance beforehand."[41] But "compared to other women in the history of the . . . Christian tradition . . . Hildegard appears as a model of restraint."[42] Her younger contemporary and eventual disciple, Elisabeth of Schönau, went into a trance during her visions, was unable to speak, and often lost consciousness when her visions occurred. Later, Teresa of Avila said that during her trances it was impossible to speak or even to open her eyes. And Catherine of Siena revealed that she was visited repeatedly by fiends uttering obscenities and tempting her with lust.[43] Hildegard's visions evidence none of these characteristics.

The British neurologist Oliver Sacks has put forward "a convincing case for Hildegard's visions and their attendant illnesses as resulting from migraine attacks."[44] Though Hildegard makes no mention of headaches (with Sacks's observation that migraines do not necessarily have to have such a symptom in order to be a migraine), the visual disturbances, nausea, rushing and roaring sensation, abdominal pain, trance-like drowsiness, muscular weakness, epileptic-like attacks, and paleness square with those attributed to Hildegard and which she herself describes.[45]

Whatever the case, her visions emphasized "The Light" or "the living Light." It is apparent that some of the visions were self-justifying, as she would appeal to their authority and not simply to her own, in order to get done the things she in particular wanted or to get things done the way she wanted. In 1136, when Jutta died, Hildegard at the age of thirty-eight was voted in by her fellow sisters as *magistra* (literally, "mistress") of the abbey. When she wanted to leave Disibodenberg and build a new monastery at Rupertsberg eighteen miles away, she was confronted by her abbot, Cuno, and the monks with opposition. Her reply was to indicate that in one of her visions God had ordered her to make the move.[46]

41. Maddocks, *Woman of Her Age*, 62.

42. Maddocks, *Woman of Her Age*, 62.

43. Maddocks, *Woman of Her Age*, 62.

44. Sacks, *Migraine*, 106–8.

45. Maddocks, *Woman of Her Age*, 63.

46. Maddocks, *Woman of Her Age*, 90–91.

Initially, when she did not share that vision, it was reported that she became blind and was so weak that she could not raise herself from her bed, let alone walk. Her visions received papal approval, when at the Synod of Trier (held from November 1147 to February 1148) Pope Eugene III and his teacher, Bernard of Clairvaux, presented and spoke in favor of, respectively, Hildegard's revelatory visions. Her visions were thereby sanctioned. Cuno and the monks at Disibodenberg undoubtedly lamented that their resistance to her desire to move and their hope that the Pope would restrain her and put her in her place had backfired. For, rather than being discredited, Hildegard had been affirmed by a synod and had the endorsement of Pope Eugene III himself. So, not only did she move her eighteen nuns and build another monastery literally from the ground up, but also "a minor local celebrity [had been born and] was suddenly famous."[47] As a result, the abbot and the monks were both the subjects of envy and its beneficiaries. They were associated with a rising star and attention and visitation to their institution would result:

> Within three years of the critical Synod of Trier, Hildegard had the world at her feet . . . and a steady stream of august international figures began to pay homage and seek counsel from this "poor little woman" who had caught the Pope's imagination so vividly.[48]

Hildegard also appealed to a vision in order to get her secretary, Volmar, to be able to go with her to Rupertsberg. It is not inaccurate to say that she bullied Cuno, saying that God had revealed to her that Volmar should not be taken away from her.[49] As another example, toward the end of her life she said that the true light overruled the order of the clergy at Mainz for her to disinter a man's body from the cemetery at Rupertsberg who had been

---

47. Maddocks, *Woman of Her Age*, 78; it was in 1147–48 that Hildegard founded her own abbey at Rupertsberg near Bingen. And then about twenty years later, in 1165, she founded an additional abbey (this one for lower class nuns) in Eibingen, also on the Rhine but on the other side near Rüdesheim.

48. Maddocks, *Woman of Her Age*, 89.

49. Godefridus and Theodoric, *Vita* 1.4.

supposedly excommunicated, possibly as a heretic. When she refused, arguing that this man had become penitent upon his deathbed and was in good standing with the church, great pressure was brought to bear on her—her nuns were forbidden to sing the Divine Office and were barred from participating in the Mass and receiving the sacrament.[50] However, this order was rescinded six months before her death in 1179.

She was not always successful in her appeal to the divine Light, to God's revelation, to achieve what she desired. When one of her nuns, Richardis of Stade, was appointed abbess at another monastery, Hildegard, who held a very special love for Richardis— "[I] bore a deep love for [this] certain noble young woman"[51]—desperately opposed that election. In this resistance she was violating Rule 2 of the Benedictine Rule, which says that neither the abbot nor the abbess should make any distinction among persons in the monastery, for equal love should and shall be shown to all. It should also be noted that Richardis was the daughter of a woman of the same name, who had helped Hildegard get Rupertsberg, and a distant cousin of Jutta, who had trained the young Hildegard as a nun.[52] Hildegard defiantly refused to let her go, justifying her disagreement by contending that God, too, in a vision, was against the move. She took her opposition all the way to the Pope, but he did not rule in her favor and informed Hildegard to let Richardis go. Hildegard reluctantly agreed. Ironically and tragically, two years later, Hildegard received a letter from Richardis's brother conveying the sad news that she had died on October 29, 1152. In a reply to Richardis's brother, Hartwig, Hildegard said that she loved Richardis with a "divine love, as indeed the Living Light had instructed me to do in a very vivid vision."[53] Hildegard was fifty-four years old at the time.

But it is not accurate to claim that her visions were simply manipulative devices to get what she wanted. In the volumes

50. Baird and Ehrman, *Letters of Hildegard*, 1:76.
51. Godefridus and Theodoric, *Vita* 2.5.
52. Maddocks, *Woman of Her Age*, 105.
53. Baird and Ehrman, *Letters of Hildegard*, 1:51.

describing her visions, Hildegard relayed divine insights she received. And very significantly for our purposes here, a good number of them spoke of the relationship between humans and the natural world. This will be discussed later.

Clearly, she was a woman ahead of her time: She found her voice at the monastery and at middle age—as previously indicated, women did not have a voice in her society, as they were either wives and mothers or nuns (or prostitutes). However, she was not theologically liberal, but rather more traditional and practical. And she was not a feminist, though modern feminists want to find in her an embryonic beginning of feminism. Instead, she had a very traditional view of women—women's passions were heated by men as women were passive by themselves. Women were more subject to the lure and temptation of lust than men. Women were vessels for men's "seed" and the only purpose of intercourse was for procreation. Analogically, women were the fields, and males were the plowmen and tillers: "A woman conceives a child not by herself but through a man, as the ground is ploughed not by itself but by a farmer."[54] For Hildegard, women were inferior, men superior. "Their roles [must] remain distinct, the man displaying manly strength and the woman womanly weakness."[55] Divorce was not to be permitted, not even in the case of adultery on the part of either husband or wife.[56] In this assertion, she contradicts Jesus's words about divorce in Matthew 19:3–13 and Matthew 5:31–32, in which he grants permission for divorce in the case of adultery.

But, at the same time, she parted company with a conservative tradition when she indicated that menstruating women could attend church, that her nuns did not have to have their heads shorn four times a year (as mandatory according to the Benedictine Rule), that nuns could show their hair and not have their heads covered and wear jewelry and crowns. In her musical morality play, *Ordo Virtutum* ("The Play of the Virtues," composed ca. 1150), she

54. Hildegard, *Scivias*, 177–78. See Thompson, "Hildegard of Bingen on Gender."

55. Maddocks, *Woman of Her Age*, 211.

56. Flanagan, *Visionary Life*, 63.

dressed her nuns in white clothing with bejeweled crowns and exposed flowing hair. This "lavish dress and immodest deportment
. . . broke St. Benedict's rules and drew adverse attention."[57] The
Rule of St. Benedict and the Rule for Nuns stipulated, "Do not
wear 'notable' clothing but rather simple in design and respectable
in color, with no embroidery or needlework."[58] And, according to
Bernard of Clairvaux, Hildegard's contemporary, "soft clothing is
a sign of moral flabbiness."[59]

Understandably, then, she was criticized by Tenxwind, the superior of a foundation of canonesses at nearby Andernach on the
Rhine, for "the manner in which Hildegard's nuns adorned themselves, as brides of Christ, with flowing hair, jewels, and crowns."[60]
Hildegard responded by quoting Scripture—rather questionably—
attributing the prohibition about jewelry and physical propriety to
married women, and not to virgins/nuns. Later, she appealed to a
vision to justify the symbolic usage of the crowns in response to a
letter from Guilbert of Gembloux, who visited Hildegard late in
her life and wrote an unfinished biography of her.[61]

Hildegard was also ahead of her time by illustrating that
a woman could be a correspondent and a writer—she wrote
"around" four hundred letters with some recent scholarship speci-
fying 373,[62] when most women (of those who could write) composed only a smattering. Hildegard "wrote letters to an astonishing
number of people,"[63] answering the questions of common people
and also representatives of all echelons of society and admonishing
fellow nuns and monks as well as popes and kings. In so doing, she
often used symbolic images, frequently drawn from nature, that
often placed judgment on the recipient. To illustrate, in a letter to
the countess Oda of Eberstein, Hildegard wrote these castigating

57. Maddocks, *Woman of Her Age*, 75.

58. Caesarius, *Rule for Nuns*, 222.

59. Maddocks, *Woman of Her Age*, 80.

60. Maddocks, *Woman of Her Age*, 79.

61. Maddocks, *Woman of Her Age*, 83.

62. Baird and Ehrman, *Letters of Hildegard*.

63. D'Evelyn, Review of *The Letters of Hildegard*, para. 1.

words: "There was a certain valley that sometimes dried up and sometimes burst forth in flowers. It did not, however, consistently produce wholesome plants, and though it was beautiful for people to see, it was not very useful for sustenance. So it is with your mind."[64]

Some of her advice and corrections were quite political. For example, although her correspondence with Emperor Frederick Barbarossa when he was elected king of Germany in 1152 was cordial—with her offering congratulations and some words of advice and his granting her an imperial charter of protection for her abbey at Rupertsberg—she began to criticize him when a papal schism developed between Frederick and the disputed successor to Pope Hadrian IV, Pope Alexander III. Frederick had supported an antipope, Victor IV, and when Victor died, Frederick appointed a successor instead of seeking reconciliation with the pope in power. What upset Hildegard was the subjection of papal authority to that of a secular ruler. So, in this "most celebrated of her quarrels," she called her "imperial patron a madman."[65]

So, though Hildegard was a woman of her time, there is clear evidence that she was also a woman ahead of her time. It was forbidden for monks and nuns to go outside the walls of the monastery and preach, and for nuns to preach at all. Chapter 36 of the Rule of St. Benedict states, "There is no necessity for the monks to go about outside [of the abbey], since that is not at all profitable for their souls."[66] And both virtue and safety were at stake for nuns.[67] So, monks and nuns "should remain within [the cloister walls] for their own safety as well as for their spiritual well-being."[68] Scripturally, the teachings of Saint Paul regarding women and their speaking and teaching incarnated in canon law also forbade women to preach. However, with papal approval she engaged in preaching outside her enclosed walls, in other monasteries and in churches

64. Baird and Ehrman, *Letters of Hildegard*, 3:4.
65. Newman, "Introduction," 15.
66. Maddocks, *Woman of Her Age*, 23.
67. Maddocks, *Woman of Her Age*, 23.
68. Maddocks, *Woman of Her Age*, 213.

(with fellow monastics and priests and nuns as audiences), and also in public (with laypersons in attendance), within four preaching tours (while she was in her sixties) between 1158–71. In fact, she preached for nearly twenty years overall. Her stated purpose in preaching was "to announce to the clergy and the people what God wanted of them."[69] Her target was also heretical sects, such as the Cathars, who were dualists, setting in opposition the soul and the body on the one hand and God and the world on the other, proposing that there were actually two gods—a good God responsible for spiritual things and an evil God who was responsible for the physical creation. In her sermons, she advocated humility, zeal, duty, and faith. The chief sins which she chided were: Corruption and injustice in decision-making among both sacred and secular leaders; indolence among church leaders; the failure of clerics to maintain celibacy (for they were interpreting celibacy narrowly and self-servingly as meaning remaining unmarried but not as forbidding the taking of mistresses and the begetting of children); loyalty to princes and kings rather than to God and obeying God (whose will, she believed, could be transmitted in sacred leaders' orders and directives); church authorities not standing up to heresy and schism; and the too-frequent practice of simony (the buying and selling of church positions).

Religious officials who stood in the crossfires of her prophetic volleys and suffered her castigations did not invoke the biblical injunction in 1 Timothy 2:12—"Permit no woman to teach or to have authority over men; she is to keep silent"—in order to put her "in her woman's place," but instead they actually invited her to preach and then sometimes wrote to her afterwards asking for copies of her sermons. Seemingly, she could preach in the first place and then get away with her scathing criticisms of persons in positions of both secular and sacred power because her reputation and fame stemmed from papal validation of her visions (Pope Eugene's "seal of approval") and endorsement of her spiritual responsibilities and work.

69. Godefridus and Theodoric, *Vita* 3.17.

In regard to these sermons, she believed that her visions—a divine light (*lux viviens*) that came to her—enabled her to understand the Bible beyond her "inadequate" education and normal comprehension:

> I saw an extremely strong, sparkling, fiery light coming from the open heavens. It pierced my brain, my heart, and my breast through and through like a flame which did not burn; however, it warmed me. It heated me up very much like the sun warms an object on which it is pouring out rays. And suddenly I had an insight into the meaning and interpretation of the psalter, the Gospel, and the other Catholic writings of the Old and New Testaments.[70]

This "insight" can be aptly illustrated by the way in which Hildegard interpreted certain Scripture passages. Genesis 1 is a chapter from the Hebrew Bible/Old Testament which was a major focus of her attention. In her approach, she was guided by the "four meanings" of the text, the "four senses of interpretation" which were common in, and defined, medieval exegesis (interpretation): First, the literal sense (What does the passage say? What are the facts?); second, the allegorical sense (What does the passage mean? What does the passage say analogically or symbolically in order to indicate what the Christian should believe?); third, the moral or "tropological" sense (What does the passage say about how Christians should live and behave? What should Christians do?); and fourth, the anagogical sense (What should one aspire to? What will happen at the end of time?). Here's what Hildegard says about the literal meaning of "And the earth was without form and void; and darkness was on the face of the deep" (Gen 1:2a):

> The earth was formless, that is to say, lacking form, and invisible, having no light because it was not yet illuminated by the splendor of light, nor the brightness of the sun, moon, or stars, and uncultivated because it had been tilled by no one, and void, that is, without order because

70. Godefridus and Theodoric, *Vita* 1.2.

it was not yet full, as it did not yet have the greenness, promise or burgeoning of plants or trees.[71]

And regarding the allegorical meaning, she explains:

All the people, that is the Jews and Gentiles, who live on the face of the deep, that is, the earth . . . were blind and deaf to the recognition of God, and empty of good works, since they did not live according to the teaching of the Son of the Highest, until he ascended to his Father. And thus on the earth, which is the face of the deep, was the darkness of unbelief, in which men lived, not recognizing God, as if they were blind.[72]

Regarding the moral meaning, she suggests:

The person who can never be steadfast in his behavior is quite formless and ever flooding like the sea . . . surrounded by dark deeds which pertain to depraved actions . . . and the body is like the face of the abyss, the soul like the abyss, because the body is visible and palpable like the face of the deep, the soul invisible and impalpable.[73]

In this instance, she does not supply a particularly anagogical or eschatological (regarding the end-time consummation of history) meaning beyond the three levels indicated. As Caitlyn Duehren has noted in discussing two of Hildegard's sermons on the visit of the three women to Jesus's tomb on Eastern morning, her regular pattern "quickly departs from the literal sense of interpretation and immediately launches into the allegorical"; it employs "an exceptional use of metaphor to creatively interpret the passage," and in this way, she "far surpasses traditional exegesis."[74] In this entire process, Hildegard claimed to be informed and educated by the divine light which came to her, enabling her to understand not just the literal meaning of a text, but also the greater and more important meaning. In this, she was able to move from the level

71. Derolez and Fronke, *Liber Divinorum,* ch. 17.

72. Derolez and Fronke, *Liber Divinorum,* ch. 20.

73. Hildegard, *Liber Divinorum,* ch. 23.

74. Duehren, "Mouth of God," 83.

of the small to the large, from the lesser to the greater, from the human to the divine, from the microcosmic to the macrocosmic.

The bringing together of microcosm and macrocosm was not only a scriptural interpretation tool, it was also the way she understood the connection between the human species and the rest of nature. "God fashioned the human form according to the constitution of the firmament and of all the other creatures, as the founder has a certain form according to which he makes his vessels."[75] Thus, "the sphere of the human head indicates the roundness of the firmament, and the right and balanced measurement of the forehead reflects the right and balanced measurement of the firmament."[76] The proportions of the human head are thereby compared with the world.[77] Thus, the created world has integrity—"harmony"—and all of it is related to God.[78]

In *Scivias*, Hildegard shares an analysis of the human body by comparing it to the structures of the universe—again, the body is a microcosm of the macrocosm of the *cosmos*. In other words, the visible and temporal are a manifestation of the invisible and eternal:

> God, Who made all things by his will, created them so that his Name would be known and glorified, showing them not just the things that are visible and temporal, but also the things that are invisible and eternal. Which is demonstrated by the vision you are perceiving.[79]

Human beings are therefore connected to the universe in an intimate and organic way. We are all "cosmic dust" as she said, echoed eight hundred years later by a comment from the late astronomer, astrophysicist, and popularizer of science, Carl Sagan (1934–1996), in *Cosmic Connections*, that "we are all made of stardust." In Sagan's *Cosmos*, he stated that "The nitrogen in our DNA,

75. Bowie and Davies, *Hildegard of Bingen*, 29.

76. Bowie and Davies, *Hildegard of Bingen*, 29.

77. Maddocks, *Woman of Her Age*, 45.

78. Maddocks, *Woman of Her Age*, 45.

79. Hildegard, *Scivias*, 94.

the calcium in our teeth, the iron in our blood, and the carbon in our apple pies were made in the interiors of collapsing stars. We are made of starstuff."[80]

Hildegard goes on, however, to accent the distinction, the prominence of human beings in the created order of things. The rest of creation of which we are a part is "lower" than humans because it was made "for us." Quoting the "Words of David on this subject," she affirms:

> "Thou has crowned him with glory and worship, and given him dominion over all the works of thy hands" [Ps 8:6–7]. Which is to say: You, O God, Who have marvelously made all things, have crowned Man with the gold and purple crown of intellect and with the sublime garment of visible beauty, thus placing him like a prince above the height of your perfect works, which you have distributed rightly and justly among your creatures. Before all your other creatures you have conferred on Man great and wonderful dignities.[81]

She brings together both ideas—that we humans are connected to the rest of creation but also above it—when she writes about "the sandy globe of the earth and what it signifies":

> And in the midst of these elements is a sandy globe of great magnitude, which these elements have so surrounded that it cannot waver in any direction. This openly shows that, of all the strengths of God's creation, Man's is most profound, made in a wondrous way with great glory from the dust of the earth and so entangled with the strengths of the rest of creation that he can never be separated from them; for the elements of the world, created for Man's service, wait on him, and Man, enthroned as it were in their midst, by divine disposition presides over them.[82]

---

80. Sagan, *Cosmic Connection*, 189–90; Sagan, *Cosmos*.

81. Hildegard, *Scivias*, 98.

82. Hildegard, *Scivias*, 98.

Thus, despite an emphasis on the connection of humans to all of nature, there is still a hierarchy (consistent and prominent in medieval thought) that humans are dominant and "over" the rest of nature, as creation was made "for man." In our time, this "dominance" has unfortunately not resulted in the blessing of creation, but in its desecration. We have exploited and plundered, trashed and polluted. Understanding that creation was made for us, we perceive its value as extrinsic or instrumental: That is, it has value only insofar as it serves us. It has no intrinsic value in and of itself.

Regarding the "dominance" of humans over the rest of creation, Hildegard draws extensively from the creation account in Genesis 1 and its language of humans having dominion and subduing the natural world. These two notions are strong and aggressive in their translation from the original Hebrew text. But they are even more so when one considers the words which lie behind the translation. "Have dominion" is *radah*, which literally means to trample. It is a word used to describe the stomping action of squishing grapes in the making of wine. And "subdue" is *kavash*, which literally means to conquer. The word is used when an Israelite had his sword against the Adam's apple of his foe and had vanquished him. And in contexts involving women, it means rape.

Certainly, Hildegard did not intend to stipulate, or even suggest, that we humans ought to trample (squish) and conquer (vanquish) nature. But the words taken by themselves can appear to recommend an attitude and action toward nature that justify misuse and abuse. If it's all there for us to use, then we will use it—in any way we want and for anything we choose. We *have* done this, and our environmental problems have been the result. When challenged, some have replied that we were given a divine mandate to do so in the book of Genesis and the very creation story that tells us who we are and how we should act.[83]

In fact, Lynn White Jr., Christian layperson and university professor, criticized his own tradition when he placed the blame for ecological problems on the doorstep of the Church. He argued that Christianity's emphasis on the "dominion" of humans over

83. For further elaboration of this point, see Cain, *Many Heavens*, 54–56.

nature, and the placement of humans at the center of the Christian worldview (human-centered or anthropocentric) resulted in the degradation and destruction of the natural world. Humans had a right to do it, even a divine mandate to do so, given in Genesis 1: "Christianity . . . insisted that it is God's will that man exploit nature for his proper ends . . . Nature has no reason for existence save to serve man."[84]

However, current biblical scholarship has for a considerable amount of time recognized two creation accounts, one in Genesis 1 (1:1–2:4a) and the second in Genesis 2 (2:4b–25). Though there are similarities in both creation stories, they are not precisely the same in content nor are they two different ways of saying precisely the same thing. Whereas humans are made in the very "image of God" in the first account (Gen 1:26–28) and created last of all as the crowning glory of creation, the male is described in the second account (Gen 2:7) as made from the dust just like every other creature (the play on words in Hebrew is 'adam from 'adamah). And here the male (ish) is made first not last, and it is the female (ishshah) who is made last after all other things were created but not found to be a suitable "helper" or partner for the male. Thus, in the second creation story there is an intimately close connection between "man" and all other created things, a closeness displayed in the Hebrew words themselves.

The second account goes on to prescribe the proper relationship, the appropriate attitude and action, between humans and the rest of creation. Here the words "dominion" and "subdue" are not found; instead, the words directive of human action are "till" and "tend" (Gen 2:15). The original Hebrew words translated as "till and tend" are 'abad and shamar. The first verb means literally "to serve" (the noun, 'ebed, means "servant") and the second means "to protect." So, here, humans are put in the garden and instructed by God to serve it and protect it.

In the opinion of Matthew Fox, these biblical words, which he believes he also finds reflected in the theological thought of Hildegard, "invite us to let go of human chauvinism. [For] God

84. White, "Historical Roots," 203.

is in every creature—not just the two-legged ones, much less the baptized ones of our race. The *cosmos* is truly a temple."[85]

Thus, the two accounts, the two creation stories found in Genesis, must be kept in creative tension and balance, and if the "image of God" means to behave as a representative of God in the world as God behaves toward it (in loving care), then being made in God's image does not confer upon humanity a special status but rather a special responsibility—to love and to care for the world. In this way, perhaps "dominion" and "subjugation" are substantially softened—and desperately need to be—by the notions of caring and protecting.

As we discovered in Hildegard, the connection between the spiritual and the material was that "the perpetual truths of the spiritual life found everyday expression in temporal objects."[86] However, as Hildegard observed and contended, human sin messes up the divine pattern in the universe. For example, the fallen angels, punished by expulsion from heaven for their sin, became a galaxy of stars.[87] We can screw up natural elements by our sinful behavior. Since humans and nature are intimately connected, whatever we do has repercussions in the rest of the nature of which we are a part: Our sin messes up things. Although Hildegard's twelfth-century Middle Ages did not know the vast pollution that, in our twenty-first century, would choke the planet and the rapacious use of resources that would threaten Earth's sustainability, her point had prophetic implications. "Unlike the rest of creation, humanity can choose injustice instead of justice; folly instead of wisdom if it cares to."[88] In short, humans can sin and mess things up. We have chosen to do so.

Hildegard also coined a word in Latin—*viriditas*—that runs throughout her written and musical works. *Viriditas* has been translated most literally as "greenness." More symbolically, it points to the vitality, the energy, the power to grow, the creative force that

---

85. Fox, *Illuminations*, 57.

86. Maddocks, *Woman of Her Age*, 156.

87. von Trotta, *Vision*.

88. Fox, *Illuminations*, 149.

is in all. Because this energy force is within everything, all things are interconnected. There is no opposition of things—such as human and non-human life on Earth, humans and nature, or God and the world. Instead, there is "an integrity that overcomes [all these] dualisms."[89]

And though God may not be reduced to nature (God's transcendence makes God greater than the creation that the Creator has made), God is within nature. That makes nature holy; that makes the creation the dwelling place of God (not completely, of course, for God's fullness lies beyond nature; but nature is fully within God). "The entire *cosmos* now rests within the bosom of the Creator."[90] Because a "green" God is within a "green" world, and that "green" world is within a "green" God, nothing is devoid of God. All things have sacred value as such. The sacred one is within nature, nature is within the sacred one, so nature is sacred within itself.

The historian Arnold Toynbee once criticized the Western belief in one God among Christians, Jews, and Muslims by indicating that a very regrettable consequence of this monotheistic worldview is the displacement of God from nature and the world. And Toynbee argued that the removal of the sacred permits the world and nature to be abused.[91] The Muslim scholar, Seyyed Hossein Nasr, has pointed to the same connection. However, he disagrees with Toynbee by saying that the belief in one God does not necessarily evict God from the world. Instead, he argues that God has never actually departed (despite our thoughts perhaps to the contrary) and is not an absentee landlord. Instead, God is present in the world, and God's signs/presence are everywhere in nature for the discerning eye to behold. Thus, it is humans who must "resacralize" nature—i.e., put the sacred back, return God to the creation, first in our thoughts and then in the way we treat nature.[92] With the awareness that God is in nature, and that therefore

89. Madigan, *Mystics*, 95.

90. Fox, *Illuminations*, 55.

91. Toynbee, "Religious Background," 141–46.

92. Nasr, "Resacralization of Nature," 270–92.

nature is sacred, we must act accordingly. To treat nature badly is to "blaspheme" God—that is, to insult the Creator who not only brought the creation into being but who also is present in it.[93]

According to *viriditas*, then, everything in nature is special, valuable, and sacred. "Greenness" or "greening power" unifies and interconnects everything as holy. We humans journey within the circle of life (Hildegard's "Cosmic Wheel") and within the embrace of the God who "embraces all."[94]

Hildegard has been crowned with the title of the first woman scientist and the first female physician. As Fiona Maddocks points out, if one were to qualify this as "one of the first," the entitlement would be accurate.[95] After having created *Scivias* in the ten years between 1141–51, Hildegard compiled two large scientific works between 1152–58—*Physica* and *Causae et Curaen*. The nine books comprising the *Physica* examine botany, zoology, metals and elements, and stones, detailing their physical and medicinal properties. For example, Book 1 of the *Physica* "contains 230 individual entries on plants, with many herbal remedies, love potions, and lust quenchers."[96] Overall, nearly a thousand plants and animals are listed. In Book 5, Hildegard records thirty-seven species of fish plentiful in rivers like the Rhine, and in Book 6, seventy-two species of birds.

Causae et Curae investigates the causes and cures of disease. Superstitious at the least, and hilarious at the most, the remedies for maladies range from: an unconscious bat tied to one's loins to heal jaundice; powdered salmon to remedy rotting gums; primrose to fight depression; a concoction of mole's blood, goose feet, the beak of a duck, and flour—or alternately drinking water in which a dead mouse has been steeped—to cure epilepsy; a mixture of rue, wormwood, and honey to correct male impotency; drinking water which contains the dried liver of a lion to aid in digestion; placing stones eaten and ejected by a pregnant mouse on a woman's navel

93. Berry, "Christianity and Survival," 149–64.
94. Uhlein, *Meditations*, 36.
95. Maddocks, *Woman of Her Age*, 147.
96. Maddocks, *Woman of Her Age*, 151.

to alleviate painful childbirth; and broth from the pulverized liver of a hamster eaten with bread to relieve lymph-node swelling.

One critic has remarked that such remedies, such "cures," are reflective of the adjective "dark" in Dark Ages.[97] However, what she is doing here that is significant for our investigation is connecting humans organically to the rest of nature. The "connection" is biological and medicinal and theological. It is biological because, since "man" is a "microcosm of the macrocosm," nature as well as the universe has a relationship to humans and *vice-versa*. It is medicinal because this relationship, properly observed, can heal humans of their maladies. It is theological because "these remedies come from God,"[98] and the study and investigation of nature is an "act of praise." "To Hildegard, a study of the bounties of earthly Creation would have constituted an act of praise no less valid than her examination of the universe and salvation in [her collection of visions in] *Scivias*. The physical world, too, has its own litany."[99] Ultimately, the creation is praiseworthy because it is the gift of God.[100]

To see this connection, one need only ponder the current use of plants in the rainforest for pharmaceuticals to assist in the soothing of maladies and the curing of diseases: 25 percent of our current medicines come from just 10 percent of the known plants in the rainforest. Current medical estimates are that 90 percent of diseases afflicting humans can be treated/cured by prescriptive drugs derived from nature.[101] The challenge today is not refusing to recognize this fact, but rather our not responding adequately to the fact that the rainforest is disappearing so quickly that we are losing potential solutions to our maladies at a rate of extinction that results in many plants dying out before they can even be catalogued and scientifically investigated. "Rainforests once covered an estimated 14% of the earth's surface. They now cover less than

97. Singer, "Scientific Views," 1–55.

98. Hildegard, *Causae et Curae*, 165.21.

99. Maddocks, *Woman of Her Age*, 148.

100. Maddocks, *Woman of Her Age*, 163.

101. "Owed to Nature."

6%. At current rates of loss, the rainforests will be completely gone in forty years."[102]

Recent musicologists have pointed out that Hildegard is known today most of all for her music. It is "her chief claim to modern celebrity," and with justification she has been designated as the "earliest named composer."[103] But as unprecedented, unique, and valuable as her compositions are, music was only a small but significant portion of her total work and her full contributions. Be that as it may, her musical productivity was truly substantial and remarkable. She is the author of seventy-seven to eighty-three compositions (depending on how one counts) in *Symphonia armonie celestium revelationum* (or simply *Symphonia*), and of the earliest enduring morality play (*Ordo Virtutum*), written ca. 1150, a century and a half before the next one would arrive on the historical scene. She believed that "music was the mirror of divine order"[104] and that "Paradise . . . is a place filled with music."[105] For Hildegard believed that music not only expressed the spiritual delight in the hearts of prophets and wise persons, it also frightened away the devil.[106]

Music, then, is to be properly understood as a part of the heavenly spheres, and humans just need to be quiet and listen to/ for it. "Hildegard, in keeping with others before and after, saw the world as a hymn of praise to God."[107] The Music of the Spheres parallels the physical and emotional makeup of human beings who in turn make their own music. The music of the heavens (what the sixth-century Roman philosopher Boethius called *musica mundane*) parallels human-made music (*musica humana*). The harmony in music points to the harmony of the universe—disparate parts all following the baton of the Creator, the divine composer, God. Hildegard repeatedly mentions that she believed that

102. "Amazon Rainforest Facts," para. 9.
103. Maddocks, *Woman of Her Age*, 187.
104. Maddocks, *Woman of Her Age*, 190.
105. Mews, "Religious Thinker," 68.
106. Newman, *Voice of the Living Light*, 68.
107. Maddocks, *Woman of Her Age*, 190.

Adam's voice was in tune with the choirs of angels before the fall and that he could hear the Music of the Spheres. As composer Sir John Tavener (1944–2013), whose "Song for Athene" was sung at Princess Diana's funeral, has remarked,

> Unless you believe in divine revelations, what I'm saying will sound like nonsense, but I believe that when God created the world, he created everything, so music is something that already exists. You just have to be very still and hear it. Plato believed that was the case. I'm not being over-pious if I say to God, "Guide me, help me." It's a kind of prayer, so therefore writing music is a kind of prayer.[108]

Hildegard was also distinctive in that she believed that God could be understood not only with stereotypical masculine characteristics but also with stereotypical feminine characteristics. So, she accented God as maternal, illustrating this by focusing on God's charity. In Book 2 of *Scivias*, Hildegard speaks of "the embrace of God's maternal love" (charity):

> Through this fountain of life came the embrace of God's maternal love, which has nourished us unto life and is our help in perils, and is the deepest and sweetest charity and prepares us for penitence.[109]

In this vein and in the same vision, she also quotes 1 John:

> By this the charity of God has appeared toward us: That God has sent his Only-Begotten Son into the world, that we may live by him. In this is charity, not that we have loved God, but that he has loved us.[110]

Some have said that this addressing the "motherhood" of God was due to the effects of maternal separation on the young child, left at the monastery at age eight.[111] But regardless, she felt com-

---

108. Interviewed in Maddocks, *Woman of Her Age*, 185.
109. Hildegard, *Scivias* II.2.4.
110. 1 John 4:9–10.
111. Maddocks, *Woman of Her Age*, 37.

fortable and very justified in referring to God (typically described in stereotypical male terms with the nouns "Father," "Judge," and "Lord" and the pronoun "He" and the possessive pronoun "His") with stereotypical female references.

It has been tempting for twenty-first-century thinkers and persons of faith to grab onto this and fortify it with references to her boldness, her leadership, and her activities ahead of her time, thereby declaring her as the first feminist or at least one of the first. This is an understandable but exaggerated appellation. Despite certain elements of "forwardness," stretching stereotypes of her time, and the freedom she enjoyed and the tenacity she displayed, she held very traditional, inherited sexist perspectives and understandings of women and men, which have been partially and previously noted. She also thought that men were "higher" in the chain of being, the hierarchy of worth and power, and women were "lower"; men were stronger, physically and morally, women weaker; men were eligible to become priests, bishops, monks, abbots, and popes, women were not; women were the descendants of Eve, through whom sin entered the world (the devil tempting the more vulnerable of the two), men were not; women were more closely connected to the earth, and to flesh, and this was manifested in women's menstrual cycles and demonstrated in their deeper carnality and greater inclination to lust; men were not.

Despite this, the "forwardness" (unusual in her time) of using feminine stereotypical language as well as masculine stereotypical language to address, and to talk to and about, God should not be underestimated. Indeed, and relatedly, as Jane Bishop, one of the cotranslators of the *Scivias* has pointed out, the content and insights of her visions are addressed to "mankind" (*homo*), meaning person/human, and not just man/male (*vir*) or woman/female (*mulier*).[112] So again, although she was a twelfth-century person in many ways, in many other ways she transcended her time period.

In conclusion, Hildegard was both faithful and unfaithful—obedient and disobedient—creative and conformist—to the Benedictine order of which she was a devotee and the traditions which

112. Bishop, "Co-Translator's Note," 56.

regulated her monastic life and thought. She upheld chastity and traditional sex and sex roles (with admonitions against fornication, masturbation, sex without the intention of procreation, and homosexuality), but also disregarded certain rules that forbade her to preach, to leave the walls of the nunnery, to take liberties with how her nuns dressed, and how she addressed God, to name just a few.

She appealed to the divine Light as a justification, a divine sanctioning, of her words and/or actions. "Hildegard consistently claimed to be acting as 'God's mouthpiece' rather than expressing her own thoughts and opinions."[113] She always insisted that she acted as God's spokesperson, pleading her own feeble femininity.[114] She was fond of saying, "I, a poor little form of a woman and a fragile vessel, say these things not from myself but from the Serene Light: People are vessels which God has fashioned for Himself."[115] But this "status emboldened her."[116] And so, the more audacious she became, the more she used this alibi of being an ignorant, unlearned, and simple woman. As we have noted, this humility—this self-effacement—was more pretense than reality.

Hildegard of Bingen was tenacious, stubborn, assertive, bold—at times aggressive and uncompromising—courageous, and in other situations, cantankerous and strident and stringent. She could be both engaging and enraging—her secretary and confessor Volmar knew the first, and they remained fast friends and confidants for nearly forty years until his death in 1173; her Abbot Cuno at Disibodenberg knew the second. He was Hildegard's superior from 1136–55 and was understandably both put-off by her and simultaneously quite envious, for she—and certainly not he—had become the marquee celebrity. Thus, their relationship involved a "tussle" throughout the years, to say the least, and to Cuno, Hildegard must have been "one tough sister" (pun intended).[117]

113. Flanagan, *Visionary Life*, 185.
114. Maddocks, *Woman of Her Age*, 74.
115. Baird and Ehrman, *Letters of Hildegard*, 2:180.
116. Maddocks, *Woman of Her Age*, 74.
117. Allen, quoted in Maddocks, *Woman of Her Age*, 263.

Hildegard was a person of her time. She was a woman ahead of time. She was "a rare feminine voice soaring above the patriarchal choir."[118] She was traditional and creative, conservative and sometimes progressive, enthralling and haughty, intrepid and irksome. Her assertions about who humans are, and can be, and what our relationship to the *cosmos* as a microcosm of the macrocosm truly is; her understanding of *viriditas* penetrating and unifying nature and all the universe; her insights about God as "Mother" as well as "Father" gifting creation to us (and therefore creation can, and ought to, praise God in gratitude); and her presenting "greenness" (*viriditas*) as the appropriate subject matter of music are all suggestive of a healthier perspective today for the relationship of humans and *humus*, between *Homo sapiens* and the creation, for humanity and nature.

On September 17, 1179, Hildegard died. Two years later, Francis of Assisi would be born. On May 10, 2012, over eight hundred years after her death, Hildegard of Bingen was finally canonized by Pope Benedict XVI.

118. Newman, "Introduction," 10.

ATTUNEMENT

The Writings of St. Hildegard of Bingen

Theological/Visionary Works

- *Scivias* [*Know the Ways*] (written 1141–51)—her first major work, twenty-six visions in three books: Book I: "Six Visions"; Book II: "Seven Visions"; Book III: "Thirteen Visions"

- *Liber Vitae Meritorum* [*Book of Life's Merits*] (written 1158–63)—a dialogue between virtues and vices

- *Liber Divinorum Operum* [*Book of Divine Works*] (written 1163–73/74)—her third theological work and last visionary writings—three parts, ten visions

Medical/Scientific Works

- *Physica* and *Causae et Curae* (written 1151–58):
- *Physica*—nine books, discussing the prevention and cure of illnesses through a detailed analysis of plants, trees, animals, metals, stones, and elements. She drew from translated works of antiquity such as Pliny, Galen, Soranus, and Isidore of Seville, though these are unnamed.

- *Causae et Curae*—takes theories cited in *Physica* further and articulates a holistic view of the world, in which illnesses are predetermined by balance and imbalance. Gender differences and sexuality are explored.

- *Lingua Ignota* [*Unknown Language*] and *Litterae Ignota* [*Unknown Writing*] (written 1150–60)—her invented language of circa nine hundred words relating most closely to scientific works and lists several plant and herb names.

Musical Works

- *Ordo Virtutum* (The Play of the Virtues) (written circa 1150)—one of the earliest surviving morality plays, consisting of eighty-two melodies; the play depicts the human soul caught between the opposing forces of the virtues and evil.

- *Symphonie Armonie Celestium Revelationum* (The Symphony of the Harmony of Celestial Revelations, or "Symphonia") (written 1140/1150)—seventy-seven poems set to a single melodic line.

Other Works

- Letters (written 1146/47–78)—nearly four hundred letters written in Latin to four popes, emperors, bishops, secular rulers, monks, and nuns
- *Pentachronon* [*Mirror of Future Times*] (compiled 1220)—an abridged collection of Hildegard's works at her most prophetic and apocalyptic, compiled by Gebeno of Eberbach.

Recommendations for Further Reading:

Duehren, Caitlyn. "From the Mouth of God: Hildegard of Bingen's Biblical Hermeneutics." *Journal of Theta Alpha Kappa* 35 (Spring 2011) 83.

Flanagan, Sabina. *Hildegard of Bingen: A Visionary Life*. New York: Routledge, 1998.

Fox, Matthew. *Illuminations of Hildegard of Bingen*. Rochester, VT: Bear, 2002.

Hildegard of Bingen. *Hildegard of Bingen: Scivias* [a collection of twenty-six of her visions]. Translated by Mother Columba Hart and Jane Bishop. Mahwah: Paulist, 1990.

International Society of Hildegard von Bingen Studies. http://www.hildegard-society.org.

King-Lenzmeier, Anne H. *Hildegard of Bingen: An Integrated Vision*. Collegeville: Liturgical, 2001.

Maddocks, Fiona. *Hildegard of Bingen: The Woman of Her Age*. New York: Doubleday, 2001.

Migne, J. P. "Saint Hildegard of Bingen and the *Vita S. Hildegardis*." *Tjurunga: An Australasian Benedictine Review* 29 (1985) 4–25; 30 (1986) 63–73; 31 (1986) 32–41; 32 (1987) 46–59.

Migne, J.-P., ed. *Vita S. Hildegardis, Patrologia Latina*, vol. 2. Translated by Anna Silva. Cambridge: Cambridge University Press, 1855.

Newman, Barbara J. "Hildegard of Bingen: Visions and Validation." *Church History* 54 (1985) 163–75.

————. *Sister of Wisdom: St. Hildegard's Theology of the Feminine*. Berkeley: University of California Press, 1987.

Newman, Barbara J., ed. *Voice of the Living Light: Hildegard of Bingen and Her World*. Berkeley: University of California Press, 1998.

Roth, Stephanie. "The Cosmic Vision of Hildegard of Bingen." *The Ecologist* 30.1 (2000) 40–42.

Ruether, Rosemary Radford. *Visionary Women: Three Medieval Mystics*. Minneapolis: Fortress, 2002.

Schipperges, Heinrich. *Hildegard von Bingen: Healing and the Nature of the Cosmos*. Munich: Beck, 1995.

von Trotta, Margarethe, dir. *Vision: From the Life of Hildegard von Bingen*. 2009; New York: Zeitgeist Films.

Chapter Two

FRANCIS OF ASSISI

The Patron Saint of Ecology

IN OUR PRESENT TIME, most persons in the United States live in cities. More than 80 percent of Americans are city dwellers, fewer than 20 percent are rural residents.[1] And in our economy, money is the agent of commerce, and few transactions are conducted through other means, such as barter.

But imagine a time when most persons lived in the country. And consider a time when it was land and not money which determined a person's wealth. The Middle Ages in European history is widely regarded as constituting the one-thousand-year time period between the fifth century AD and the fifteenth century AD, or more specifically, from the time of the fall of the Western Roman Empire in 476 to the Renaissance and the Age of Discovery in 1492. At the start of this time period, the majority of persons lived in rural areas. Princes served as feudal lords, and castles and monasteries dotted the rural countryside.

Beginning in the early eleventh century, there was a major shift from people living in rural areas to moving into cities. "For

1. Rural areas contain 19.3 percent of the population (about sixty million people), Census Bureau Director John H. Thompson stated in a report on December 8, 2016.

the medievalist, the urbanization phase, which began around the year one thousand, marks a crucial turning point."[2] Urban historian Peter Clark explains this by noting that urban communities drew persons to them by "chances"—the chance for more employment opportunities, the chance for increased social mobility, the chance for more freedom of thought and action.[3] Added to this, increased agricultural productivity generated surpluses of products and people (labor), so that large numbers of farmers migrated to the cities. And finally, the establishment of political, religious, and cultural institutions strengthened the growth of cities.

Francis's Italy experienced the highest rate of urbanization in all of Europe.[4] Italy's cities grew at double the rate of the cities of other countries,[5] with Milan, Florence, and Venice—along with Paris in France and Grenada in southern Spain—being the five highest populated cities in Europe with over one hundred thousand residents each.

Walls were then necessarily constructed around such cities for protection and defense, and one repercussion of this, since walls were expensive to build and therefore needed to be of shorter rather than longer circumference, was to compress the population density and thereby persons lived closer to one another. In this new situation, poor persons could no longer grow crops on land around them or gather food from the land of others and thus have access to nutrition; as a result, poor persons were found on the streets, and others encountered them in ways that had been less noticeable in rural life. Although poverty had previously existed, of course it now became much more obvious. So, the "chances" for improvement also contained risks—the risk of greater poverty, the risk of higher mortality rates due to disease, and the risk of greater economic and political instability.

Accompanying this urbanization was the reintroduction of money as a means of exchange. Used in the ancient world as an

2. Blockmans, "Urbanization," 16.

3. Blockmans, "Urbanization," 16.

4. Bosker, "Cities in Italy," 6.

5. Bosker, "Cities in Italy," 6.

agent of commerce, money made a reappearance in the late medieval period. Consequently, gold and silver coins became the measure of wealth and no longer the ownership of land. As historian William Cook has pointed out, no one in this time period sifted soil through his hands and proclaimed, "I'm rich." Rather, persons could count their coins in their money bags at night on their beds, and in this way assess and acknowledge their wealth.[6]

The monetary economy underwent great expansion from 1180–1280, the period in which Francis's life is placed (1181/1182–1226). An investigation into the literature of this time period shows that "coffers" and "money bags" and "purses" are mentioned with far greater frequency than ever before, and a survey of archaeology of the time shows that the remains of keys were also found in abundance. This clearly points to containers for money, the new measure of wealth, and to the need to protect it under lock and key.[7]

Among other issues, the reinstitution of money raised the problem of "interest." The Bible had clearly forbidden usury, the practice of lending money and charging interest:

> Exodus 22:25—If you loan money to my people, to the poor among you, don't be like a creditor to them and don't impose interest on them.

> Deuteronomy 23:19—Do not charge a fellow Israelite interest, whether on money or food or anything else that may earn interest. You may charge a foreigner interest, but not a fellow Israelite, so that the Lord your God may bless you in everything you put your hand to in the land you are entering to possess.

> Leviticus 25:36—Do not take interest or any profit from them, but fear your God, so that they may continue to live among you.

---

6. Cook and Herzman, *Medieval Worldview*, chs. 8 and 9.
7. Araies and Duby, *Revelations of the Medieval World*.

Leviticus 25:37—Remember, do not charge interest on money you lend him or make a profit on food you sell him.

Punishments for those who did charge interest on money—the usurers—were laid out, with implications for both earthly and heavenly punishment: The Second Lateran Council in 1139 condemned usury as "ignominious." The Third Lateran Council in 1179 went further: Canon 25 leveled three severe "capital" decisions. The first was excommunication for "open usurers," the church's categorization of the usurer during this period, thus exiling him from the Christian community. The second was the prohibition against burial in Christian cemeteries. And the third was the forbidding of offerings made by usurers, thus keeping them from the practice of public charity, expected from faithful Christians who would follow Jesus's example and the Church's teaching.

Despite this legal and spiritual prohibition against lending money for interest, larger "up front" amounts of money were required to fund commercial projects for business and to promote trade. And the lenders necessarily had to concern themselves with the risk of such loans, for ships could sink and the cargo would be lost or there could be other reasons for the borrower to default on the loan. So, the church wrestled with "what to do with money" and what to do "with charging interest."[8] In a feudal, agrarian economy, these were not issues; but in an urban money-based economy, they became issues.

The working out of these issues, which resulted in the—at least partial—endorsement of the money economy, granted a remarkable rise in prosperity, and persons became fixated on money. Historians have indicated that materialism then abounded, and money emerged as the new "idol" of the time.[9]

In addition, though the early church had been pacifistic, initially eschewing war and fighting and killing, there rose a popular Code of Chivalry one thousand years

8. Cook and Herzman, *Medieval Worldview*, chs. 8 and 9.
9. Cook and Herzman, *Medieval Worldview*, chs. 8 and 9.

later. How should the church understand and respond to
this movement which developed largely between 1170–
1220? Villagers and workers in feudal lands owned by
lords and barons were subjected to taxes and rents, and
these obligations were paid in terms of labor rendered,
crops grown, and also by soldiers provided. Lords and
barons were responsible, "obliged," to provide the same
to the king. The Code of Chivalry provided a halfway
measure regarding war: Fighting was understood as a
just action, guided by bravery, courtesy, honor, and gal-
lantry toward women. The knight would commit to the
following rules to regulate both behavior and thought,
known in later literature as the "Ten Commandments of
Chivalry":

1. Thou shalt believe all that the church teaches and thou
   shalt observe all its directions.

2. Thou shalt defend the church.

3. Thou shalt respect all weaknesses, and shalt constitute
   thyself the defender of them.

4. Thou shalt love the country in which thou wast born.

5. Thou shalt not recoil before thine enemy.

6. Thou shalt make war against the infidel without cessa-
   tion and without mercy.

7. Thou shalt perform scrupulously thy feudal duties, if
   they be not contrary to the laws of God.

8. Thou shalt never lie, and shalt remain faithful to thy
   pledged word.

9. Thou shalt be generous, and bestow money and gifts
   on others.

10. Thou shalt be everywhere and always the champion of
    the right and the good against injustice and evil.[10]

---

10. Gautier, *La Chevalerie*, 26. Although Gautier wrote this long after
the Middle Ages, it is a summary of the values and virtues he found in the
literature of the medieval time of knights and chivalry, especially French literature since France developed substantially the notion of knights, chivalry,

Thus, the Church became more tolerant toward war and regarded it as an effort which defended the Christian faith, which helped the Church maintain peace. In part, the knight would defend those who could not defend themselves. In this way, battle—and even wars—could be justified as noble efforts to protect the weak, the unprotected, and the defenseless.

It is not surprising, then, that a young boy growing up in this *ethos* would dream of becoming a knight in the same way as a boy today might dream of becoming a professional athlete, an astronaut, or a military hero. Francis himself would be subject to this dream of his time. And there would be opportunity for him to become so involved, because there were frequent rivalries among cities in Italy which led to armed conflict. In fact, in 1202, he engaged in the intercity warfare between his native Assisi and nearby Perugia, was captured and held as a POW for a year, became ill, and then was ransomed. In addition, a later foray into battle would be abandoned when he had a dream beforehand and returned home, coming to believe that there was "another way": the way of peace.

Also, the early church had prized martyrdom as a badge of courage. Indeed, some of the attraction of Christianity to non-Christians in its beginning centuries was provided by the devotion and loyalty of its followers in times of persecution by the Roman Empire. But ever since the fourth century, Christianity had no longer been judged illegal as a threat to the security and stability of the empire and had no longer been despised as unpatriotic to the government (since Christians refused to worship the gods who protected the empire and refused all oaths of royal loyalty save to God). Instead, Christianity had become the preferred religion, and then the official religion, of the empire under Emperors Constantine and Theodosius I. Indeed, the Roman Empire became known now as the *Holy* Roman Empire.

This original zeal for martyrdom was now transformed into enthusiasm for wresting the Holy Land away from its Muslim conquerors, and the Crusades were born, the first beginning in 1095. In fact, the Fourth Crusade (1202–4) would be undertaken when

---

and courtly romance.

Francis was in his early twenties and was intended to recapture Jerusalem from Muslim control. And halfway through the following crusade—the Fifth Crusade (1217–21)—he would journey to Egypt where the crusaders were laying siege to the city of Damietta and struggling against the Muslim forces of Al-Malik al-Kāmil (the Sultan of Babylon—"Babylon" being the section of Cairo in which he had his capital). Despite the opposition of Cardinal Pelagius, the religious leader of the crusade, and John of Brienne, the secular leader, Francis crossed enemy lines and met with the Sultan and preached to him. Although Al-Malik al-Kāmil was impressed by Francis's courage and elocution (giving Francis many going-away gifts), he did not convert. But Francis had attempted this conversion, not by the sword but by the Word of God.

So, it was into this time of abrupt transition and of paramount issues that Giovanni di Pietro di Bernardone (renamed Francesco or "Francis"—"Frenchman"—by his father) was born in either 1181 or 1182 (the precise date is unclear.) He was born in Assisi, a small and relatively unimportant village slightly over one hundred miles north of Rome. Today, the visitor cannot be but profoundly struck by the hordes of tourists who visit the town out of devotion and to honor Saint Francis and by the natural beauty of the town's hillside location and the Umbrian Valley below.[11] His father was a wealthy cloth merchant, arguably the richest businessman in town. Francis was the eldest child of his father, Pietro di Bernardone, and his French mother, Monna Pica, and was positioned to be the heir apparent to the family's textile enterprise.

Early on, Francis spent his time enjoying his position and status in town. He loved finery and wearing the latest of fashion. He also reveled in going to parties and was regarded by his young friends as the life of the party. Therefore, he was rich and popular and "[presided] over a band of like-minded young men devoted to the pursuit of happiness."[12] Influenced by his time, he desper-

---

11. Share, "Spirituality and Mysticism," 60.

12. Thomas of Celano, *First Life*, 2; Thomas of Celano, *Lives of St. Francis*; see within esp. *Anonymous of Perugia*, 3–6; *Legend of the Three Companions*, 2–3; *Remembrance of the Desire of a Soul*, 7.

ately wanted to be a soldier—ultimately a knight—and figured that he would be knighted if he performed well in battle. By contrast, as previously mentioned, he was captured and imprisoned in a nearby town, and a second attempt to join a crusade under Walter of Brienne also proved unsuccessful.[13]

Francis returned in June of 1205 from this second try, disappointed and the butt of the jokes and mockery of his friends, resuming his "playboy" lifestyle.[14] However, he found the cloth business to be unsatisfying and began to spend time in solitude in caves outside Assisi in prayer. According to tradition, while also praying in 1206 inside a church in Assisi, the Chapel of San Damiano, he heard a voice coming to him from the crucifix which implored him to "Rebuild my church" (some versions render it, "Go and restore my house").[15] Taking this command seriously, which he believed to have come from Jesus himself, Francis set about begging for stones and other building materials from the citizens of Assisi. His father, perhaps understandably, became concerned, for this was not proper behavior for a member of the entrepreneurial merchant class.

Francis also made a pilgrimage to Rome and threw money in St. Peter's tomb through a grate protecting and distancing the tomb from the worshipper. This act of charity was not completely fulfilling, so when Francis went outside the church, he persuaded a beggar on the square to exchange clothes with him and begged for the remainder of his time there.

When he returned to Assisi, he went to a neighboring town, carrying with him some of his father's cloth. He decided to sell this cloth and the horse upon which he had been riding and brought the money back and gave it to one of the priests to assist in the renovation of the church of San Damiano. His father was dismayed and became irate by his son's action, so in January or February 1206, he brought Francis to court in front of Bishop Guido, essentially to disinherit him and to cut him out of the will. When

13. Thomas of Celano, *First Life*, 4.
14. Thomas of Celano, *First Life*, 10–12.
15. Thomas of Celano, *Remembrance of the Desire of a Soul*, 10.

Francis was confronted and asked to return to his father what was his father's, he stripped himself naked on the town square, gave his clothes to his father, and declared that he now had only one father, his "heavenly Father." The bishop took his own cloak and covered the nude Francis with it. Legend has it that Francis then ran from the square out into the snow of winter, joyfully singing songs in French.[16]

Earlier and typically in his life, Francis had avoided lepers completely and stayed at a distance, actually holding his nose as he passed by the leprosaria where they were confined. But now, when he unexpectedly met a leper, he had a change of heart and chose to live among those afflicted with this scourge of the Middle Ages. His conversion from what he had been to what he was now was so profound that he no longer seethed with contempt for lepers, but instead held compassion (suffering-with) for them, not even superficial sympathy. He would comment at the very end of his earthly days that living with and ministering to the lepers was the most joyful episode and action of his life.

Francis then committed to living a life of poverty ("marrying" Lady Poverty), standing over against the increasing materialism and greed of his century and the intensified obsession with money and rising wealth. This was a radical alternative to the prevalent *ethos* of his society, and eventually others were drawn to him and his values and lifestyle. A small, but growing, movement resulted.

To legitimate the new movement, Francis and eleven others[17] journeyed to Rome in 1209 to receive papal authorization from Pope Innocent III for the group. Afterwards, they were to be known as the Order of Friars Minor (*Fratres Minores*)—the "Order of Beggar Brothers of Assisi," a humble nomenclature—or simply as "Franciscans." *Jongleurs* ("Jesters" or "Fools") was the term that Francis himself would later use, and he wanted them to be known

---

16. Chesterton, *St. Francis*, 42.

17. I.e., symbolically Jesus and the eleven disciples with Judas left out, or symbolically the twelve disciples with Francis as one of them, while some traditions say twelve others (i.e., symbolically Jesus and the disciples returned to twelve with Matthias added to replace Judas).

as *Jongleurs de Dieu* ("Jesters of God").[18] Not surprisingly, Francis saw himself as "the court fool of the King of Paradise."[19]

Francis, then, consistently referred humbly to himself as a "fool," and alternately as the "most wretched of sinners," believing that God had sent him into the world in this way in order to show God's ways.[20] He also referred to himself as the "stupid son of Pietro di Bernardone."[21] This was partially understandable, as he had no university education, was not a scholar, and had not fully mastered Latin. In fact, it is said that in writing five Latin words, Francis would make two mistakes![22] In addition, he had not been ordained to the priesthood, and beyond this, what he represented was something new and not the predominant and popular way to embody the Christian faith and live out the Christian life.

In this, he believed he was following the model of his Lord, Jesus, who not only said, "Those who exalt themselves will be humbled, and those who humble themselves will be exalted" (Matt 23:12; Luke 14:11), but who also embodied these words in the life that he lived. In fact, the apostle Paul points to the example of Christ *par excellence* when Paul shares one of the oldest hymns of the church which praises Jesus's humility:

> Have this mind among yourselves, which is yours in Christ Jesus, who, though he was in the form of God, did not count equality with God a thing to be grasped, but emptied himself, taking the form of a servant, being born in the likeness of men. And being found in human form he humbled himself and became obedient unto death, even death on a cross. Therefore God has highly exalted him and bestowed on him the name which is above every name, that at the name of Jesus every knee should bow, in heaven and on earth and under the earth, and every

18. Chesterton, *St. Francis*, 35–38.
19. Chesterton, *St. Francis*, 39.
20. Armstrong et al., *Francis of Assisi*, 18.
21. Martin, *Salvation Scenes*, 9.
22. Martin, *Salvation Scenes*, 103; Habig, *Omnibus of Sources*, 18.

tongue confess that Jesus Christ is Lord, to the glory of
God the Father.[23]

It should be added that Francis saw himself as the "worst of
sinners," not because he truly was, but because he felt he had not
used adequately and fully the gifts that had been given to him. So,
his humility, his foolishness, was acted out not as excessive self-
effacement—a refusal to acknowledge any self-worth at all—but
rather as relentless self-criticism. He joked playfully, but seriously,
calling his body, "Brother Ass."[24]

This model of humility, of relentless self-criticism, and of
holding one's self to the highest standard possible is at great odds
with life in today's world. The prevalent *ethos* of American society
revolves around one's ego at the very center of the individual's life
and all aspirations and activities are chosen and undertaken to
satisfy one's wants and one's greed. "Enough" seems to be always a
little more than what one has ever had, and "entitlement" assures
the individual that he or she deserves whatever he or she wants.

Just as nature is seen in anthropocentric terms (i.e., it is
"there" to satisfy whatever and however much we want), so one's
place in the scheme of things is seen in egocentric terms, at the
very center (or completely at the top), and everything exists in
order to serve and satisfy the individual's cravings and obsessions.

A lot (some would argue most) of our cravings and obsessions
are for "things," more things, the latest things, the most expensive
things, the things we believe will make us feel special, happy, and
satisfied. As the popular bumper sticker reads, "He wins who dies
with the most toys." And so, we want toys.

This leads inevitably to greed and leaves any sense of Francis's "poverty" behind. Surprising to most, a case can be made
that the dominant religion in the United States is not Christianity.
Although the 2017, year-long-researched Gallup Poll indicated
that 75 percent of Americans identify with various groups within

---

23. Phil 2:5–11.

24. Habig, *Omnibus of Sources*, 459.

Christianity,[25] if by "religion" one means that which concerns a person most ultimately—something that is most important to that person—then God can be that ultimate concern of a person or something else—like money—can be. "Money is his god" is a way of describing such a non-theistic "ultimate concern."[26]

Based on this definition and distinction, it can be argued that "consumerism" is the most dominant "religion" currently in the United States. Shopping malls—not churches, synagogues, mosques, or temples—have become our sacred spaces; salespersons and cashiers have become our priests; and our credit cards have become our sacraments.

This has spilled over into some actual church settings in the form of what's been termed the "prosperity gospel." In part, this "gospel" proclaims that God wants people to be rich. And toward that end, if individuals will only contribute to the coffers of churches led by prosperity pastors, God, in turn, will bless those contributors many times over beyond the level of their gifts. Mennonite and Professor of History of Christianity at Duke Divinity School Dr. Kate Bowler has written a definitive book entitled *Blessed: A History of the American Prosperity Gospel*.[27] And in her *New York Times* article, "Death, the Prosperity Gospel, and Me," she shares the following: "I am a historian of the American prosperity gospel. Put simply, the prosperity gospel is the belief that God grants health and wealth to those with the right kind of faith. I spent 10 years interviewing televangelists with spiritual formulas for how to earn God's miracle money."[28]

The prosperity gospel is one theological perspective on why some people make it and some don't. It is an explanation for why some people have it (money, possessions, affluence) and why some don't. It is an understanding that allows those who have, to say

25. Newport, "2017 Update"; see Newport, *God Is Alive*.

26. "Religion is the state of being grasped by an ultimate concern, a concern which qualifies all other concerns as preliminary and which itself contains the answer to the question of the meaning of life." Tillich, *Dynamics of Faith*, 1.

27. Bowler, *Blessed*.

28. Bowler, "Death, the Prosperity Gospel," para. 3.

to others—including those who are without—"I am blessed. God gave this to me as a reward for my faith and/or my giving to God's causes/ministry/ministers. Don't blame me. Again, I have been blessed by God."

In contrast to this "unfettered accumulation" theology, which promises that if you follow the rules and God's will, God will reward you (materially, financially, relationally), Francis followed Jesus's "call to surrender all." Indeed, Francis believed that giving everything away/up would provide the antidote to the expanding money economy of his time, which bred a "frenetic spirit of commerce" in Italy and an "insatiable desire to make money" in Assisi.[29] So, poverty became Francis's most treasured principle, and he took a vow of total poverty.[30] In fact, he was so concerned about the negative impact of having and hoarding money that, according to the Order of 1223, the definitive set of rules for the Franciscan friars, the *Jongleurs de Dieu* were not even allowed to *touch* money, let alone possess it! Appealing to the Gospel lesson of Matthew 10:7–10, Jesus's words are quoted: "Take no gold for your journey. . . no purse . . . nor two tunics, nor sandals."

In response to the virulent stress today on "having" and "getting," Christian theologian Jay McDaniel acknowledges American culture and its/our addiction to consumerism, but then provides helpful insights and recommendations. His "Ten Healing Alternatives to Consumerism" are as follows:

> Living lightly on the Earth and gently with each other is much more important than appearance, affluence, and achievement;
>
> Healthy living requires not only creativity, action, and good work but also rest and relaxation, so that our work can be productive rather than compulsive;
>
> It is much more important to be a good parent, be a good neighbor, and be a good person than to have a successful career, particularly if "success" is defined purely in monetary terms;

29. Martin, *Salvation Scenes*, 4.
30. Martin, *Salvation Scenes*, 12.

Truly good work does not consist in making money or in exploiting natural resources, but rather in serving others, often without being noticed;

Helping others, and dwelling in solidarity with people in need, is more important than prosperity in the suburbs;

Compulsive shopping is a symptom of disease, not a cure for depression;

The world is not a global marketplace, but rather a gorgeous planet, filled with many creatures, each of whom is loved by God on its own terms and for its own sake, and each of whom contains God within;

Happiness lies not necessarily in "having my needs met," but rather in living simply and in service to others;

The universe is a communion of subjects, not a collection of objects;

We are not on our own, because the universe is enfolded within an ultimate grace that renders questions of "success" and "failure" irrelevant.[31]

Several of these alternatives accent and recover for our time the outlook and values of Saint Francis—living lightly (simple living) benefits our own spirituality and well-being; riches are not the measure of success; meaning and happiness come from serving, not from making money; and we live in a universe of subjects, not objects. This last point will be discussed below.

Nature for Francis (according to biographer Bonaventure's *Life of Francis*) provided a "series of footprints to God." As historian William Cook has pointed out, "If you probe deeply enough into the world, what you are going to find is God."[32] "For Francis, nature forms an arrangement that reflected the 'beauty of God.'"[33] Thus, the heavens and all life on Earth were regarded by Francis as manifestations of the power and glory of God, "the Most high, all powerful, good Lord."[34]

31. McDaniel, "Living from the Center."

32. Cook and Herzman, *Medieval Worldview*, 27; see Sorrell, *St. Francis*, 39–54.

33. Share, "Spirituality and Mysticism," 79.

34. Saint Francis, "Canticle," 1.

Francis is an example of someone who prayed in nature and discovered more about God and himself through the practice of contemplative prayer in nature. Francis spent a third to half of each year praying in nature and the wilderness, living in hermitages, caves, under lean-to's, on mountainsides, and he interspersed this with preaching. There was something about that experience of being intimately related to creation itself that helped him grow more fully into the mystery of God. And that's what we are desperately in need of today, because we are so alienated from the earth and from ourselves.[35]

For Francis, then, nature was replete with the presence and the thumbprints of God. The father of modern science, Sir Francis Bacon, would later affirm the same insight in the seventeenth century. For Bacon, nature was a "second Bible." The "first" Bible, of course, was the written book, while the second source of revelation was nature, "a living book." The seeker could learn about God by consulting both books—reading the Bible and observing nature. Bacon claimed, though, the Bible was primary. However, ignorance of the second book—nature, or "creation"—could be likened to a "second fall of humanity."[36]

It is interesting that the world's second largest religion—Islam—with 1.8 billion adherents—also affirms this discernible presence of God in nature/creation. In Islam, there is confidence that, in exploring more intensively and extensively the creation, one comes to know more fully and more deeply the Creator. The "handiwork of God" is revealed to those who are able to read the "signs." In fact, the verses of the revealed, definitive, holy book of Islam—the Qur'an—are called *ayats*. And the signs of God's fingerprints in the creation—for example, the beauty, harmony, and organization of nature, both at the macroscopic and the microscopic levels—are also called *ayats*. The connection is clear, both in the original Arabic and in the English translation: Each of them is revelatory, and through both of them we learn more about God.

35. Warner, "St. Francis," 25.
36. Hendry, *Theology of Nature*, 54–56.

This view of nature as good, as containing the evidence for God's existence and of God's work and presence in the creation, stood in sharp contrast to the prevailing view of nature in the Middle Ages. In large part due to the frequent and devastating onslaught of diseases like the bubonic plague, nature was viewed as evil, and sometimes as "the domain of the Devil." In fact, nature was not only dangerous to one's body, it also threatened the security of a person's soul.[37]

It is noteworthy that Francis's perspective—a "minority opinion" at the time—would be one which in later history would undergird and prompt the intentional investigation of nature and the resultant accumulation of knowledge. Though "fallen," nature was originally created as good by God (see Genesis 1), and an appropriate response to a good-though-fallen creation was to learn about it, in the process learning more about the God who created it. Barbara Brown Taylor, contemporary theologian and Episcopal priest, puts it this way: "Earth is so thick with divine possibility that it is a wonder we can walk anywhere without cracking our shins on altars."[38] Therefore, nature is something to be valued, not something to be either ignored or dismissed.

Further, and as we have noted before, Francis strongly believed that nature is composed of subjects, not objects. Theologian Paul Tillich (1886–1965) argued that the chief problem in our view of nature, and consequently our relationship to it and actions taken in it, is that we have "thingified" nature.[39] That is, we have reduced nature to "things," to objects. Thusly objectified, these items do not have any value in themselves, but receive value only in their usefulness to us humans. Having no intrinsic value, they may be used for whatever purpose suits us, wise or foolish, sustainable or unsustainable.

The famous Jewish philosopher Martin Buber (1878–1965) made an important distinction between relationships that are understood as between two subjects (I-Thou relationships) and

---

37. Merchant, *Death of Nature*, 81. See also Merchant, "Environmentalism."

38. Taylor, *Altar*, 15.

39. Tillich, *Systematic Theology*; see Pan-chui, "Paul Tillich," 233–49.

relationships that are understood as between a subject and an object (I-it relationships). In the first type of relationship, there can be high, positive regard; equality; respect; and a "Golden Rule" interaction ("Do to others what you would have others do to you.") In the second type of relationship, there is inequality, with the subject positioned "above" the object. Here the "golden rule" is "I will do to this object what I wish because it is inferior to me, beneath me, and therefore is only there to serve my interests, be they selfish or not."[40]

Francis of Assisi preceded Buber by over seven hundred years in "seeing" nature as filled with subjects—brothers and sisters—as realities to whom we ought to relate as I-Thou rather than as I-it. In short, since God was the Father, all living things were siblings. We see this in what he wrote, most particularly and especially, "The Canticle of the Creatures," or, as it is sometimes called, "The Canticle to Brother Sun and Sister Moon," and we see this in his actions in the world.

"The Canticle to Brother Sun and Sister Moon" was written by Francis at the Church of San Damiano in the spring of 1225, about eighteen months before his death.[41] It was written in Italian rather than official, scholarly Latin. Here is a translation of the Canticle into English by the Franciscan friar, Benen Fahy:

> Most high, all-powerful, all good, Lord!
> All praise is yours, all glory, all honor
> And all blessing.
> To you alone, Most High, do they belong.
> No mortal lips are worthy
> To pronounce your name.
> All praise be yours, my Lord, through all that you have made,
> And first my lord Brother Sun,
> Who brings the day; and light you give to us through him.
> How beautiful is he, how radiant in all his splendor!
> Of you, Most High, he bears the likeness.

40. See Buber, *I and Thou*, for a complete treatment of this point.
41. Brother Leo, *Mirror of Perfection*, 100.

All praise be yours, my Lord, through Sister Moon and Stars;
In the heavens you had made them, bright
And precious and fair.
All praise be yours, My Lord, through Brothers Wind and Air,
And fair and stormy, all the weather's moods,
By which you cherish all that you have made.
All praise be yours, my Lord, through Sister Water,
So useful, lowly, precious, and pure.
All praise be yours, my Lord, through Brother Fire,
Through whom you brighten up the night.
How beautiful is he, how bright! Full of power and strength.
All praise be yours, my Lord, through Sister Earth, our mother,
Who feeds us in her sovereignty and produces
Various fruits with colored flowers and herbs.
All praise be yours, my Lord, through those who grant pardon
For love of you; through those who endure
Sickness and trial.
Happy are those who endure in peace,
By you, Most High, they will be crowned.
All praise be yours, my Lord, through Sister Death,
From whose embrace no mortal can escape.
Woe to those who die in mortal sin!
Happy are those She finds doing your will!
The second death can do no harm to them.
Praise and bless my Lord, and give him thanks,
And serve him with great humility.[42]

The Canticle has been regarded as "the jewel and the crown, as it were, of Franciscan literature,"[43] and "the highest expression of Francis's nature spirituality."[44] This prayer of praise to God as the Creator "pinpoints creation's unity as fraternal."[45] That is,

42. Habig, *Early Biographies*, 130.
43. Doyle, *Song of Brotherhood*, 39.
44. Share, "Spirituality and Mysticism," 158.
45. Share, "Spirituality and Mysticism," 129.

creation is understood as unified, and nature is one interrelated entity, because it is a family, a family headed up by God. Given this metaphor, God is the Father, and we are the children, but with all other members of nature. Family members may, and ought to, address each other as "brothers" and "sisters."

And family members ought to treat one another with respect and with honor. It is interesting, as Mary Elizabeth Share has noted, that Francis uses courtly language when he addresses the sun as *messor lo frate sole* ("Sir Brother Sun," "My lord Brother Sun").[46] Earlier we noted Francis's desire to be a knight and his historical context in the atmosphere of chivalry. And by this use of courtly language, Francis is indicating that the sun, and all other entities in creation, should be cared for with respect, loyalty, and honor.

In "The Canticle," then, Francis saw the rest of nature as subjects in their own right, as siblings—fellow children—of the Father who created all. This perspective was horizontal and non-hierarchical; there was no vertical ranking—nothing was located above or below anything else. Strikingly, this perspective was a departure from the widespread and common outlook on the natural world in Francis's time. The medieval worldview saw a "pyramid" with God at the very top and the angels located below. Humans were ranked under the angels, with men prioritized over women. Then came the animals further down, followed by plants, and at the lowest level were rocks and minerals.

This is not the way that Francis "saw" animate and inanimate subjects. As fellow children, all subjects are equal. There is no ranking, no subordination of one subject—one species—to another. There is a "democracy" of all in God's creation.[47] This is quite similar to the perspective of indigenous peoples, groups around the world that have preceded the modern civilizations that we know today. These indigenous people located in the United States are called Native Americans.

Hundreds of individual tribes and separate cultures make up the "Native American" portion of the North American continent

46. Share, "Spirituality and Mysticism," 135.
47. White, "Historical Roots," 1206.

in which the United States resides. Consequently, cataloguing beliefs and rituals in order to find areas of commonality and similarity is a daunting task. Be that as it may, several general themes can be discerned. The survival of these hunter-gatherer groups hinged on an intimate knowledge of the natural world. Knowing nature's rhythms and cycles, dangers and secrets, allowed them to coexist within nature. Nature was not a "thing" that was distant from humans, but rather a "web," a community, in which humans are an important but equal strand. Misreading or abusing nature would be disastrous. Other entities—animate or inanimate—were subjects, "brothers" and "sisters." All other groupings were "peoples," as this quality and status were "givens." Groups were distinguished by the group reference name preceding the common noun, "people." Because of this, there were "deer people," "fish people," "bird people," and "human people." As different peoples, animate and inanimate entities (though Native Americans regard all of nature as "alive," whether animate or inanimate), one was to refer to each other as "brother" and "sister"—for example, "Brother Eagle" and "Sister Sky."[48]

Beyond this, the "Great Spirit," however conceived and however named, permeated all of the natural world. Therefore, nature was imbued with spirit and was regarded and revered as sacred. We human people do not own the land; rather, it belongs to the Great Spirit. We humans are "custodians," not "owners."[49] In a famous letter/speech, attributed inaccurately to Chief Seattle, a tribal leader of the Suquamish and Duwamish tribes of the Pacific Northwest, these various components of the Native American perspective are articulated. Here is an excerpt from that letter/speech, as it appears in former Vice President Al Gore's book, *Earth in Balance: Ecology and the Human Spirit*.

> How can you buy or sell the sky? The land? The idea is strange to us. If we do not own the freshness of the air and the sparkle of the water, how can you buy them?

48. Jeffers, *Brother Eagle*.

49. Cain, *Down to Earth*, 77–83; see Krech, *Ecological Indians*; Hughes, *American Indian Ecology*; Neihardt, *Black Elk Speaks*.

Every part of this earth is sacred to my people. Every shining pine needle, every sandy shore, every mist in the dark woods, every meadow, every humming insect. All are holy in the memory and experience of my people . . . If we sell you our land, remember that the air is precious to us, that the air shares its spirit with all the life it supports. The wind that gave our grandfather his first breath also received his last sigh. The wind also gives our children the spirit of life. So if we sell you our land, you must keep it apart and sacred, a place where man can go to taste the wind that is sweetened by the meadow flowers. Will you teach your children what we have taught our children? That the earth is our mother? What befalls the earth befalls all the sons of the earth. This we know: The earth does not belong to man, man belongs to the earth. All things are connected like the blood that unites us all. Man did not weave the web of life, he is merely a strand in it. Whatever he does to the web, he does to himself. One thing we know: Our God is also your God. The earth is precious to Him and to harm the earth is to heap contempt on its Creator.[50]

The Swiss missionary, doctor, musician, and theologian Albert Schweitzer (1875–1965) came to see the natural world in much the same way. While crossing the Ogooué River in Gabon in west central Africa, he came to the realization that all of life is worthy of reverence. Every species possesses a "will-to-live," so "I must regard other life than my own with equal reverence."[51] Such a regard, such an ethics of reverence for life,

makes no distinction between higher and lower, more precious and less precious lives. It has good reasons for this omission. For what are we doing, when we establish hard and fast gradations in value between living organisms, but judging them in relation to ourselves, by whether they seem to stand closer to us or farther from us? This is a wholly subjective standard. How can we

50. Gore, *Earth in Balance*, 159.

51. Schweitzer, "Reverence for Life," 185; see Schweitzer, *Philosophy of Civilization*, 309.

know what importance other living organisms have in themselves and in terms of the universe?[52]

Schweitzer goes on to argue that this is a religious outlook and found in the ethics of Jesus:

> The ethics of reverence for life is the ethics of Jesus, philosophically expressed, made cosmic in scope, and conceived as intellectually necessary. The great error of earlier ethics is that it concerned itself only with the relations of man to man. The real question is, however, one concerning man's relations to the world and to all life which comes within his reach. A man is ethical only when life, as such, is holy to him, that is, the lives of plants and animals as well as the lives of men. Moreover, he is ethical also only when he extends help to all life that is in need of it.[53]

Here, Schweitzer is, unconsciously perhaps, reflecting the perspective of Francis on the basic and necessary regard and respect—reverence—for all of creation.

As has been demonstrated, we see this in what Francis, and later Schweitzer, wrote. And we also see this in Francis's actions in the world. The resources about Francis in this regard are replete with stories. These stories clearly combine history and legend.[54] But, at their basic level, their intent is to express adoration for, and honor the value of, this extraordinary figure, Francis of Assisi. Several of them illustrate adequately the point:

> Francis was traveling through the Marches of Ancona and the same brother [Brother Paul] was gladly accompanying him when he came across a man on his way to market. The man was carrying over his shoulder two little lambs bound and ready for sale. When blessed

52. Schweitzer, *Reverence for Life*, 47.

53. Schweitzer, *Life and Thought*, 126.

54. Scholars have long noted the hyperbole and accretions that have become attached to these episodes in Francis's life. While they may not always present facts rooted in actual history, they do convey the historical appreciation for St. Francis.

Francis heard the bleating lambs, *his innermost heart was touched* (I Kings 3:26) and, drawing near, he touched them as a mother does with a crying child, showing his compassion. "Why are you torturing my brother lambs," he said to the man, "binding them and hanging them this way?" "I am carrying them to market to sell them, since I need the money," he replied. The holy man asked: "What will happen to them?" "Those that buy them will kill them and eat them," he responded. At that, the holy man said: "No, this must not happen. Here, take my cloak as payment and give me the lambs." The man readily gave him the lambs and took the cloak since it was much more valuable. The cloak was one the holy man had borrowed from a friend on the same day to keep out the cold. The holy man of God, having taken the lambs, now was wondering what he should do with them. Asking for advice from the brother who was with him, he gave them back to the man, ordering him never to sell them or allow any harm to come to them, but instead to preserve, nourish, and guide them carefully.[55]

Nor was Francis's concern limited to "higher" species. Even a "lowly" worm, in Francis's worldview, deserved and received his compassion, for he picked them up and put them in a safe place.[56] Common flies were referred to as "brother."[57] He also loved bees, providing wine or honey for them so that they would survive the winter.[58] Beyond this, he also favored cicadas. One of the well-known stories from the early sources is of a duet between Francis and the cicada with whom he had made friends.[59] He also sang duets with the nightingale and other birds.

Speaking of birds, Francis had a special relationship with them: According to available sources, he was filled with compassion when he saw a young man who had caught some doves and

---

55. Thomas of Celano, *First Life*, 79; see Habig, *Saint Francis,* 1:293–97.

56. Thomas of Celano, *First Life*, 80.

57. Thomas of Celano, *Francis Trilogy*, 75, 77; Brother Leo, *Mirror of Perfection*, 24.

58. Thomas of Celano, *Francis Trilogy*, 165.

59. Thomas of Celano, *Francis Trilogy*, 171.

was carrying them off to sell. Francis begged the young man to give him the doves, and when he did, Francis held the birds close to his chest and then sent them off, asking them, "Why did you allow yourselves to be caught?"[60]

Among birds, he especially loved larks: "Sister lark is a religious and humble bird . . . While flying, she praises the Lord very sweetly, like [that] which is religious . . . and [her] way of life is always in heaven and [her] intention is always for the praise of God."[61]

Francis's "sermon to the birds" has captured popular attention more powerfully than any other incident in his life, and it is found in several of the sources (especially in the biographies of Francis by Thomas of Celano and Saint Bonaventure). Since in Francis's view all of creation has a duty to love and praise God, he admonished a flock of birds in the woods—

> My brother birds, you should greatly praise your Creator, and love Him always. He gave you feathers to wear, wings to fly, and whatever you need. God made you noble among his creatures and gave you a home in the purity of the air, so that though you neither sow nor reap, He nevertheless protects and governs you without your least care.[62]

Francis also held empathy toward fish. A fisherman on the Lake of Rieti presented Francis with a large tench (carp family) as he sat in the boat. Francis addressed it as "brother" and at once slipped it over the side into the water. The fish lingered about the

60. Bronforte, *Little Flowers*, 22.

61. Brother Leo, *Mirror of Perfection*, 113.

62. Thomas of Celano, *First Life*, 58; Saint Bonaventure, *Major Life*, 12:3; Bronforte, *Little Flowers*, 16. However, Francis disliked ants because he believed they betrayed a mistrust in God by being too diligent in providing for the future, storing up provisions in their "barns" (Vian, *Sayings of Brother Giles*, 7). Of course, Francis's emphasis on Lady Poverty meant that he wanted to avoid storing up treasure and providing for the future. The ants are therefore a paradigm of what he disliked. He did not dislike the ants, *per se*, who, after all, could not behave in any other way, but he disliked the people symbolized by the ants.

boat, "drawn by love," until Francis "said a prayer"[63] or "blessed it."[64] Then it swam away.

One of the other famous stories has to do with a wolf. It is presented here in its complete form so that the full impact of the story may be enjoyed:

> There was in Italy the town of Gubbio, a prosperous vil-
> lage that had a great problem. A wolf was eating their
> livestock, and attacking the people. Nothing the towns-
> people did protected them from the wolf. Never had
> they seen such a fierce predator. He killed a shepherd,
> then the shepherd's brother and father when they went
> out to deal with this menace. The next morning the town
> was abuzz with the story told by the shepherd's mother
> and sisters. The mayor of Gubbio announced he would
> send three of his best guards to find and slay the wolf
> that very afternoon. At dusk the townspeople could hear
> shouts and clashing of metal from the woods. Then it was
> quiet. The guards had met the wolf. Late in the night, the
> only survivor of the encounter struggled into the anx-
> ious town and collapsed. After he was revived, he told
> his tale of their fight with the fierce and powerful wolf.
> As the story rushed through town the wolf grew larger
> and more ferocious. Fear was in the eyes of everyone
> in Gubbio. Children were kept close by, weapons at the
> ready, and the defenses of the town raised. The mayor
> consulted with his advisors and decided to see if Francis
> of Assisi could help them. They had heard that he could
> talk to animals and that God talked to him. Several brave
> messengers were sent to find Francis and ask him for his
> help. They had the good fortune to find him in Assisi
> at the house of Bernardo Quintivalle, his first follower.
> They told him of the tragic attacks of the wolf and how
> the frightened people were almost in a state of siege.
> They thought Francis was the only one who would be
> able to help them. They begged the simple holy man to
> help and implored him to come with them right away.
> Francis was moved by their plight and wanted to do what

63. Thomas of Celano's account of the story in *First Life*, 61.
64. Bonaventure's account of the story in *Major Life*, 8.8.

he could. He said they could leave in the morning and they should eat and rest with his Brothers that night. After dinner, they prayed with Francis for a solution and slept that night with hope in their hearts. Dawn found them walking down the hill from Assisi on their way to Gubbio. In time, they arrived at the woods near the town. The messengers pointed to where the wolf had slain the two guards not far from the road. They stayed in a tighter group as they hurried the rest of the way, watching for the wolf. The gate to the town was opened as they arrived and was quickly closed behind them. The entire town followed Francis to the town square where the Mayor eagerly met them. They went into the town hall to eat and discuss what Francis would do with the wolf. The mayor wondered what Francis could do with such a challenge. The mayor hated that wolf. He knew the men who were killed and their families. One of the guards was a cousin to the mayor's wife. If he were younger, he would have led the guards after the wolf. He wanted Francis to strike the wolf dead or send him to the town of Spoletto, their old enemy. Either would satisfy a need for revenge and stop the attacks. Francis listened as the mayor described what had happened to their peaceful town. He had much empathy for the families of the victims and wanted to meet the wolf and hear his story, too. Francis stated that the next morning he would go to the woods where the guards had been killed to see if he could find the wolf. That night he prayed for the wisdom to find a solution that would benefit everyone. Early the next morning, refreshed and confident this would work out, Francis was accompanied by the townspeople to the gates of Gubbio. They wished him well and retreated to their homes, worried that Francis would share the fate of the shepherds and guards. He walked on to the woods, ready to engage the wolf. As he neared the first stand of trees, the wolf appeared and began to stalk Francis. His slow, deliberate steps, the walk of a predator, announced his intention. He drew nearer and nearer, closing in a circle around the holy man from Assisi. Seeing the wolf, Francis felt a connection. He made the sign of the cross and called the wolf to meet him in peace under the grace of the Lord.

The wolf watched as Francis came closer. "Come Brother Wolf, I will not hurt you. Let us talk in peace." The wolf froze in mid-step. The wolf struggled with doubt and uncertainty. Finally, understanding that Francis meant him no harm, the wolf walked to Francis and sat back on his haunches, ready to listen. Francis told the wolf that he had come from Gubbio and described what the townspeople were experiencing because of the wolf's actions. He described the pain and resentment they held toward the wolf. "How did this come to happen?" Francis asked the wolf. "Why did you kill the livestock and people?" The wolf told Francis his story. He had been left behind by his pack because he was injured and couldn't keep up. He could only catch prey that didn't run fast, like sheep and goats. He really preferred to eat deer and rabbits, but, with his injured leg, that was out of the question. He explained to Francis that all he wanted was to eat when he was hungry. Francis implored him to explain his actions. The wolf continued. The first shepherd he had killed was trying to protect his flock and the wolf had no choice but to fight back and kill him. That afternoon two more men came after him and instinct took over. He quickly killed them, leaving their bodies where they fell. The next day the three guards came hunting him. He was only defending himself when he fought them. Two were slain. As the third man was no longer a threat, he let him go. Francis could see that the wolf was only acting to fill his needs. He had made unfortunate choices that affected people of whom he knew nothing. Through Francis, the wolf was able to feel the pain of the people in Gubbio and he felt remorse. He was sorry for the pain he had caused, but he needed to eat. What could he do? Hours passed as Francis prayed. The wolf watched closely, not fully understanding what was taking place, but sensing that Francis believed he felt remorse at having caused such pain. When Francis emerged from his contemplation, he quietly suggested an answer to the dilemma. It was a suggestion that could meet the needs of both the town and the wolf. He proposed to the wolf that the townspeople could feed him and, in return, the wolf would stop killing the people and their livestock. The wolf thought this would work well for him, but worried the people would still want to kill him. Francis understood the wolf's concern and assured him he would present the idea to the townspeople in such a way that he would be forgiven and welcomed into the town. He knew they could let go of their fear and hate if they saw the wolf ask for forgiveness and accede to a peaceful relationship. Francis extended his hand. The wolf showed agreement by placing his paw in Francis's hand. Saint Francis and the wolf walked back to Gubbio.[65]

Francis's reverence for nature/creation also included plants/flowers. Francis told the brother who took care of the garden not to cultivate all the ground in the garden for vegetables, but to leave a piece of ground that would produce wild plants, that in their season they would produce "Brother Flowers."[66]

An old and well-known story in China makes the same point about the value/subjective nature of all living things. In this tale, an emperor asked a famous painter to paint a picture of a rooster for him. The painter assented but said that it would take a long time. After a year, the emperor reminded him of his promise. The painter replied that after a year of studying the rooster, he had just begun to perceive the surface of its nature. After another year, the artist asserted that he had just begun to penetrate the essence of this kind of life. And so on, year after year. Finally, after ten years of concentration on the nature of the rooster, he painted the picture, a work described as an inexhaustible revelation of the divine ground of the universe in one small part of it: a rooster.[67]

For the European Francis and the Chinese painter, all creatures and living things had dignity because of their value as fellow subjects. And for Francis, this dignity, value, and subjecthood had an ultimate divine source: God was the source of all creation, ranging from the lowliest of creatures to the highest of heavenly bodies. Therefore, for Francis, inanimate objects as well were considered

65. "Saint Francis & the Wolf."

66. Armstrong et al., *Francis of Assisi*, 88; see Brother Leo, *Mirror of Perfection*, 118.

67. Kirkpatrick, "Paul Tillich."

as subjects; consequently, we humans have a kinship with all of creation—Brother Sun, Sister Moon, Brother Fire, Sister Water, Brother Wind, Sister Bird, Brother Wolf, and Sister Earth.[68] So, he would avoid walking where his washbasin had been emptied.[69] Out of respect and reverence for him who was called "The Rock," he would step with care on stones.[70] When faced with medical care of his face through cauterization by fire, he appealed to it as "Brother Fire." In another case, when Francis was sitting too close to a fire and his clothes ignited, he refused to have the fire put out, saying, "Do not hurt Brother Fire."[71] Thus, for Francis, "All creatures, whether worms or birds, water or rocks, trees or flowers . . . were an outward sign of divine grace."[72]

All these things were not "veils of illusion, concealing the Most High, but rather, signs revealing and making a bridge, as it were, to the God of light and glory. For [Francis] they were sacraments."[73] Of course, the Roman Catholic Church, the Eastern Orthodox Church, and a fair number of Protestant churches are familiar with the word "sacrament." In general usage, the term officially refers to "an outward and visible sign of an inward and spiritual divine grace," an invisible grace contained in a visible vessel, something divine or spiritual contained in something physical or material.[74]

For Francis, nature as a whole was a sacrament, a manifestation of the spiritual in the physical, the divine in the material. Greek Orthodox theologian Elizabeth Theokritoff has addressed this same insight. Using the central place of the "icon" (a pictorial image of a significant holy personage like Jesus or one of the saints) in that tradition, she makes the same point: icons are "windows

68. Thomas of Celano, *First Life*, 81; St. Francis, "Canticle of the Creatures," 6.

69. Brother Leo, *Mirror of Perfection*, 118.

70. *Remembrance of the Desire of a Soul*, 165.

71. Brother Leo, *Mirror of Perfection*, 116.

72. Share, "Spirituality and Mysticism," 88.

73. Share, "Spirituality and Mysticism," 88.

74. *New Catholic Encyclopedia*, 13.479.

into the Divine," in that they are made of wood and paint but transport the viewer to another level of reality and experience.[75]

As a result, nature is sacramental, "iconic," and is "more" than just the physical, the material. The divine, God, is present in it, and therefore, it is holy. As holy, the creation contains the Creator (not totally, because God is greater than the creation) and must therefore be treated with respect, reverence, humility, and care. Treating nature with disrespect, abuse, and exploitation is blasphemous (i.e., an insult to God).[76]

A theocentric view (God at the center), then, contrasts, and could correct, our anthropocentric (humans at the center) view of today. Our current view places humans at the center of the worldview and takes God out of the picture, thereby removing the sacred from nature. Because of this desacralization, nature is vulnerable to human dominance and degradation.

Returning to Francis's life, at the favorite of his sites of solitude, Mount LaVerna, in August and September 1224, Francis received the *stigmata*, the five signs of the suffering of Christ in answer to his "famous wish that he know both the suffering of Christ and the love Christ held for all."[77] He would die two years later, and was not alone when Sister Death came to him: Clare of Assisi was with him. She was a younger contemporary of Francis, born in 1193 into the feudal aristocracy of a family with higher noble status than Francis's. On Palm Sunday, at the age of nineteen, she had come to Francis and renounced her privileged station in life. Francis then cut her hair, and she joined a convent of nuns. A "Second Order"—the Order of St. Clare or the "Poor Clares"— would later be established so that women could follow the Franciscan ideals. Clare ministered to Francis on his deathbed; he had humbly requested for that purpose the floor of the Portiuncula Church. She indicated that he died as if falling asleep. The month

75. Theokritoff, "Orthodox Church," 63–79; Theokritoff, "Sacramental Life," 505–24.

76. Berry, "Christianity and Survival," 149.

77. Share, "Spirituality and Mysticism," 68.

was October, the day was the 3rd, and the year was 1226; Francis was but forty-four years old.

Not quite two years after his death, he was canonized as a saint on July 16, 1228 by Pope Gregory IX. 751 years later, in 1979, Pope John Paul II named him the patron saint "of those who promote ecology."[78]

78. Warner, "Patron Saint," 25.

Recommendations for Further Reading:

Armstrong, Edward A. *Saint Francis: Nature Mystic*. Berkeley: University of California Press, 1973.

Boff, Leonardo. *Saint Francis: A Model for Human Liberation*. New York: Crossroad, 1982.

Chesterton, G. K. *St. Francis of Assisi*. New York: Doubleday, 1990.

Cron, Ian Morgan. *Chasing Francis: A Pilgrim's Tale*. Grand Rapids: Zondervan, 2013.

Delio, Ilia, et al. *Care for Creation: A Franciscan Spirituality of the Earth*. Cincinnati: St. Anthony Messenger, 2008.

Habig, Marion A., ed. *Saint Francis of Assisi: Omnibus of Sources, vol. 1*. Quincy, IL: Franciscan Press, 1991.

House, Adrian. *Francis of Assisi: A Revolutionary Life*. Mahwah: Paulist, 2001.

Martin, Valerie. *Salvation Scenes from the Life of St. Francis*. New York: Vintage, 2001.

Nothwehr, Dawn M. *Ecological Footprints: An Essential Franciscan Guide for Faith and Sustainable Living*. Collegeville: Liturgical, 2012.

Share, Mary Elizabeth. "The Spirituality and Mysticism of Nature in the Early Franciscan Tradition." PhD diss., University of South Africa, 2004.

Sorrell, Roger. *St. Francis of Assisi and Nature*. New York: Oxford University Press, 1988.

Saint Bonaventure. *The Life of St. Francis*. Mahwah: Paulist, 1978.

Chapter Three

Taigu Ryōkan

The Great Fool of Mount Kugami

IMAGINE YOU ARE A young child in a small village in a country far away. Each day your parents awaken you from the single room you share with your other siblings. Your mother makes a delicious breakfast for you of rice and some small pieces of fish that your father caught the night before. It is not a school day, so after doing your chores, you are free to play. You know that your friends will be waiting a short distance down the road, so you set out to meet them. As you walk, you suddenly see them ahead of you, so you wave to them and begin to move faster, eventually running to join them. And then as you arrive to where your friends are waiting, you look up and you see a thin, elderly man approaching the group. As he gets closer, you see that he is wearing the same tattered robe which has been mended countless times.

You recognize him, of course, for he is the same man who regularly comes to your village from a hut on a nearby mountain, carrying only a single begging bowl in his hand. Whatever the adults can spare they will give to him, perhaps in order to receive spiritual gain by providing him food or maybe just to send him on his way so he will have something to eat.

You remember even more so that he is the man who loves to play games with you and the other children. Maybe today he will play that bouncing ball game with you again—he always carries a silk ball (or two) concealed inside the sleeve of his one modest garment. And he loves to play hide-and-seek. You join in with the others. They call out his name as he walks steadily and surely toward you.

"Ryōkan-san [Mr. Ryōkan], Ryōkan-san, please come play with us."

And play with you he does, laughing and joking and teasing and hiding until you hear the call of your parents telling you to return home for lunch. Here is one of his poems rehearsing his playing ball with you children:

Early spring
The landscape is tinged with the first
fresh hints of green
Now I take my wooden begging bowl
And wander carefree through town
The moment the children see me
They scamper off gleefully to bring their friends
They're waiting for me at the temple gate
Tugging from all sides so I can barely walk
I leave my bowl on a white rock
Hang my pilgrim's bag on a pine tree branch
First we duel with blades of grass
Then we play ball
While I bounce the ball, they sing the song
Then I sing the song and they bounce the ball
Caught up in the excitement of the game
We forget completely about the time
Passersby turn and question me:
"Why are you carrying on like this?"
I just shake my head without answering
Even if I were able to say something

how could I explain?
Do you really want to know the meaning of it all?
This is it! This is it![1]

Much beloved by Japanese youngsters and adults in his time and ours, Ryōkan loved children and playing with them. When they would see him coming, they would tease him constantly by shouting, "Ryōkan, you are as skinny as the first sardine of the season," and then run to him. He, in turn, would rivet their attention by pretending to be dead and allowing them to cover him with leaves. Or he would slowly tilt backwards until he had fallen to the ground, much to the shrieks of delight from the children.

He also loved to play hide-and-seek with the children. One tale that every current Japanese child knows is that, on one occasion, Ryokan ran to hide and make the children find him. He chose a haystack. Hours went by and the children simply could not locate him. Tiring of the game, they went home. A couple of adults went by the haystack and noticed Ryōkan hiding therein. "Ryōkan, what are you doing there?" they asked. Ryōkan put his finger to his lips and admonished them to be quiet lest the children be able to find him.

Today, Taigu Ryōkan, that monk, is a household name in his native Japan. In an extensive survey conducted approximately fifty years ago by the Japanese government, 99 percent of the grade school students recognized his name and knew some of his poetry and the humorous, legendary stories that surround him.[2] In fact, in the early part of the last century, there was a dynamic "boom" in attention to Ryōkan and his poetry. That interest went beyond school children and the circle of scholars, teachers, and professional poets to encompass the general public. Indeed, Ryōkan's reputation has morphed through the years from that of a local poet-monk who lived in northern Japan to a national cultural hero.[3] And so, in contemporary Japan, bookshelves are jammed

1. Translated by Abé and Haskel, *Great Fool*, 132–33.
2. Abé and Haskel, *Great Fool*, 20.
3. Abé and Haskel, *Great Fool*, 3.

with hundreds of books on Ryōkan and his poetry, and a plethora of tourist buses take native Japanese and foreign tourists to historic sites associated with him. Perhaps Ryokan's recognition and popularity could be compared in the United States to the familiarity of poets and writers such as Mark Twain, Maya Angelou, Walt Whitman, Emily Dickinson, Robert Frost, Danielle Steele, and Stephen King.

Ryōkan was born in 1758 and given the birth name Eizō Yamamoto (山本栄蔵 Yamamoto Eizō). His birthplace was in the village of Izumozaki in the province of Echigo (now known as Niigata Prefecture) in northern Japan on the island of Honshu. This province lies in the heart of Japan's snow country and has historically received cold weather and a lot of precipitation during the winter. That frosty beauty typically carries over to the other seasons as well. "A scenic spot, with panoramic ocean views, Izumozaki was known in Ryōkan's day as a haunt of artists and writers."[4] Thus, like Saint Francis of Assisi, Ryōkan lived in a beautiful area. And therefore, perhaps predictably, like Francis, Ryōkan was enamored with the natural world. Izumozaki was in economic and political competition with a neighboring seaport community, Amaze, which would eventually eclipse it and dominate the industries of transferring gold from ship to horseback, rice growing, and fishing.

It took a hardy person to live in this area of Japan, and people in Izumozaki had to brave the cold and work hard to make ends meet. Ryōkan's family, however, was prestigious and rich, as his father, Shinzaemon Yamamoto, was the hereditary village headman (a sort of "mayor"), and a poet himself who wrote under the pen name of "Tachibana I'nan."[5] His father had a passion for the *haiku* poetry of Matsuo Bashō, and desired a recovery and rebirth of Bashō's work. Traditional Japanese *haiku* poetry consists of a three-line poem with seventeen syllables, written in a five/seven/five syllable count and often focusing on images from nature. Matsuo Bashō (1644–1694) was the most famous poet of the Edo

4. Abé and Haskel, *Great Fool,* 4.
5. Abé and Haskel, *Great Fool*, 5, 259.

period in Japan, which lasted from 1603–1868 and is sometimes also called the Tokugawa period.

Ryōkan was the eldest of four sons and had three sisters. Early on, he was trained in Confucian ethics. This meant he was schooled in the ideals of moral character and associated ethical virtues. The typical ethical virtues were *dao* (the moral way people should act in human relationships in society), *junzi* (literally, being a "gentleman," but perhaps best understood as being a "superior person"—"superior" not in a prideful or arrogant way, but in a highly moral way), and *ren* (empathy or compassion). He also studied Chinese literature and Chinese poetry in a city several miles northeast of his hometown. But Ryōkan was also prepared, as the eldest or "number one" son, to follow in his father's footsteps by becoming a village headman-in-training at the age of sixteen (recall that Saint Francis was also groomed to inherit the textile industry of his family). It was assumed that at age eighteen he would succeed his father.

It should be noted, and has been by several Japanese historians of the area, that Ryōkan's father was a better poet than he was an administrator. As a result, the village of Izumozaki suffered from administrative incompetence, and Ryōkan's father eventually lost his political position to a rival family. Years later, he would end his life through committing suicide by jumping into a river. The backstory is that his father had travelled to Kyoto to present a work to the government denouncing political intrigue and corruption, and had then committed suicide, apparently to call attention to his protest. The year was 1792 (some sources say 1795) when Ryōkan arranged the funeral and subsequent memorial services and then set out on a religious pilgrimage that lasted several years.

But some years beforehand, as a young teenager, and like Saint Francis, who preceded him by almost six hundred years, Ryōkan was a young "dandy," who ran around fully self-absorbed and totally self-interested. He confesses this in one of his poems:

> When I was a lad,
> I sauntered about town as a gay blade,
> Sporting a cloak of the softest down,

And mounted on a splendid chestnut-colored horse.

During the day, I galloped to the city;

At night, I got drunk on peach blossoms by the river.

I never cared about returning home,

Usually ending up, with a big smile on my face, at a pleasure pavilion![6]

However, like Saint Francis before him, Ryōkan felt he was not suited for an inherited position as village headman in the shogun's government. So, he renounced his position and status and decided to become a Buddhist monk. The details prompting his decision are historically obscure and unavailable. What is known is that he shaved his head and went to study at a Sōtō Zen Buddhist temple,[7] Kōshōji, in the nearby rival city of Amaze. While at this temple, Ryōkan met a mendicant/itinerant Buddhist priest, Zen Master Tainin Kokusen (1723–91), who was the teacher of Ryōkan's teacher at the temple. Ryōkan was impressed by his demeanor and his teaching, so, at age seventeen, Ryōkan went to live and study at Kokusen's temple, Entsuiji, in Okayama Prefecture (adjacent to Hiroshima Prefecture at the southern end of the island of Honshu), and became his disciple.

Ryōkan studied and practiced with Kokusen for twelve years, until the Master died. He had received the name "Taigu Ryōkan" from Kokusen when he "graduated" and was believed to have attained enlightenment—Ryōkan ("broad-hearted, generous and

6. Stevens, *Dewdrops*, 3. It should be noted that a "pleasure pavilion" is not a brothel, but a "beautiful place," typically an auxiliary structure attached to a main building and often referred to in Japanese as *gemmyo* or "mysteriously beautiful." Shogun Ashikaga Yoshimitsu (1358–1408) described his pleasure pavilion as *gemmyo-tei*, or "the arbor of mysterious beauty."

7. Sōtō is one of the two major schools in Japanese Zen Buddhism, and Rinzai is the second; Zen emphasizes meditation (*zazen*) and the experience of enlightenment (*satori*); Sōtō meditation practitioners face the wall, while Rinzai face away from the wall; Sōtō sitting sessions last longer, thirty to forty minutes, and the Rinzai sessions are shorter, twenty to twenty-five minutes; Rinzai emphasizes *koans* (a paradoxical anecdote or riddle, used in Zen Buddhism to demonstrate the inadequacy of logical reasoning and to provoke enlightenment) in a more formal fashion than Sōtō does.

kind-hearted") and "Taigu" ("great fool") together meant "broad-hearted, generous fool." Kokusen also gave the following poem to Ryokan, who cherished it for the entirety of his life:

> Ryōkan! How nice to be like a fool
> for then one's Way is grand beyond measure
> Free and easy, letting things take their course—
> who can fathom it?
> I therefore entrust to you this staff of wild wisteria
> Whenever you lean it against the wall
> Let it bring the peace of a noonday nap.

Like Saint Francis before him, Ryōkan considered himself a fool, but in his case, the great fool of Mount Kugami, to which he would eventually move. For, following Kokusen's death, Ryōkan went on a pilgrimage lasting almost five years and then decided to return to his hometown area where he had grown up. He found an empty hut halfway up the mountain and began living there, supporting himself by begging in the villages below. Ryōkan lived this hermit life from around the age of forty to his death thirty-four years later in 1831. In those three-and-a-half decades, he became a masterful poet whose work has been translated into many languages, and also a master calligrapher whose work is now considered as unparalleled.

Like Saint Francis, he eschewed money. When someone tried once to give him money, he retorted, "What would I do with that?" And as was the case with Saint Francis, Ryōkan criticized the religious establishment of his time. Whereas Francis had found fault with the degree to which the church had coopted the society's obsession with materialism, greed, and money at a time of economic boon, Ryōkan attacked the practice of Buddhism in Japan. He criticized pride, insincerity, finery, and erudition with no concrete expression in action (i.e., "knowing" but not "doing").

> (Untitled)
> Talk is always easy
> Practice always hard

It's no wonder people try to make up for
their lack of hard practice with easy talk
But the harder they try, the worse things get
The more they talk, the more wrong they do
It's like pouring on oil to put out a fire
Just foolishness and nothing else.[8]

(Untitled)
The sun sets, and all living things cease to stir
I, too, close my brushwood gate
A few crickets begin to chirp
The color of grasses and trees has faded
Burning stick after stick of incense
I meditate through the long autumn night
When my body gets cold, I put on more clothes
Practice hard, fellow students of Zen!
Time is gone before you realize.[9]

It has been said that merely reading and talking about Zen
Buddhism is like going to a restaurant and eating the menu, for
conversation can be no substitute for hard endeavor. Instead, it
has to be practiced and worked on. Becoming familiar with the
literature and discussing the experience of others is no substitute
for intentional effort in awakening one's own true "buddha nature"
(the capacity within each of us to achieve enlightenment and in
this way become a "buddha"—literally, one who is "awake," one
who is "enlightened").[10]

Unlike Jesus of Nazareth, Ryōkan did not compose, nor did
his disciples leave us, a tract of his teachings. There are no Four
Gospels, no collection of Jesus's "beatitude-sayings," nor any
reputed collection of Jesus's teachings.[11] There is no *Hadith* re-
porting his words and his actions like that regarding the Prophet

8. Abé and Haskel, *Great Fool*, 247.

9. Abé and Haskel, *Great Fool*, 156.

10. Stevens, *Dewdrops*.

11. Called Q (*Quelle*) in Christian New Testament scholarship.

Muhammed, no *Lotus Sutra* (one of Ryōkan's favorite Buddhist scriptures) detailing his additional teachings like was done for those of Siddhartha Gautama the Buddha. True, some friends and acquaintances recorded some brief stories and remembrances of their relationship with him, but these were not in any sense lengthy and detailed biographical accounts. Thus, there are no specific tracts and compendia in which the explicit teachings of Ryōkan are presented and detailed.

As a result, Ryōkan's observations and insights about life and nature come to us in and through his poetry. And our observations and insights about him come from the same source. Like Jesus of Nazareth's teachings (parables), Ryōkan's teachings (poems) are enveloped in the context of the natural world. For example, Jesus teaches humans about dealing with anxiety by advising, "Look at the birds of the air; they do not sow or reap or store away in barns, and yet your heavenly Father feeds them . . . Who of you worrying can add a single hour to his life?"[12] And Ryokan teaches persons to get beyond themselves by suggesting in this poem,

> The rain has stopped, the clouds have drifted away,
> and the weather is clear again.
> If your heart is pure, then all things in your world are pure.
> Abandon this fleeting world, abandon yourself,
> Then the moon and flowers will guide you along the Way.

Ryōkan's poetry regularly and consistently evokes sensory connection with the natural world. As scholar Meng-hu has illustrated, all five senses are engaged—seeing, hearing, smelling, tasting, and touching. He offers the following analysis of this connection between our senses and the images in Ryōkan's poems:

12. Matt 6:26–27.

Visual:	river shimmering like silk trees white with peach blossoms fluttering sparrows flickering fire in a hearth glimpse of fireflies in the night books of poetry scattered on the floor
Aural:	monkey cries from a mountaintop far-off pounding of rice freezing rain at night village dogs baying at the moon cry of the *hototoguisu* [the Japanese cuckoo bird] frogs chanting in a pond cry of a deer to its mate
Olfactory:	dried leaves or wood chips burning slowly in a hearth fragrance of wild chrysanthemums or plum blossoms scent of cedar and pine carried by the wind an empty room filled with incense smoke a bowl fragrant from rice of a thousand offerings
Taste:	pure water from a temple well or spring freshly picked vegetables basket of fresh mushrooms seaweed winter greens weak tea and thin soup warm sake taros in a pot with salty miso

Tactile:	night air fresh and cool; a cool breeze at the window
	old fingers mending a tattered robe
	robe moist with dew
	tossing a ball with village children
	shivering cold in an unheated hut[13]

In terms of understanding Ryōkan, sharp disagreements have emerged regarding his religious status: did he attain the ultimate spiritual goal of his Buddhist faith tradition—enlightenment—or did he not? Some modern scholars such as Sōma Gyofū, Hasegawa Yōzō, and Tanigawa Toshirō hold that Ryōkan was completely enlightened. But these scholars ignore the poems in which Ryōkan expresses his suffering, whether through depression or loneliness or deprivation. And they do not deal with his poems which reflect his drinking to what many might consider excess. Instead, they accent the poems that point to Ryōkan's position *beyond* these quite normal human conditions and temptations in the world. Here are some examples of his poems which lend themselves to the point-of-view of these scholars:

Truly, I love this life of seclusion.
Carrying my staff, I walk toward a friend's cottage.
The trees in his garden, soaked by the evening rain,
Reflect the cool, clear autumnal sky.
The owner's dog comes to greet me;
Chrysanthemums bloom along the fence.
These people have the same spirit as the ancients;
An earthen wall marks their separation from the world.
In the house volumes of poetry are piled on the floor.
Abandoning worldliness, I often come to this tranquil place—
The spirit here is the spirit of Zen.

If someone asks
My abode

13. Meng-hu, "Zen Poetics," para. 14.

I reply:
"The east edge of
The Milky Way."
Like a drifting cloud,
Bound by nothing:
I just let go
Giving myself up
To the whim of the wind.

Finished begging my food in a ramshackle town
I return to my home among the green hills
The evening sun drops behind the western peaks
A pale moon lights the stream that runs by my door
I wash my feet, climb onto a rock
Burn incense and sit in meditation
I am, after all, a Buddhist monk
How can I let the years just drift uselessly by?

A Buddhist monk of the old school
I hid myself on Mount Kugami
I don't recall how many springtimes ago
I've worn out countless pairs of robes
But my staff has never left my side
Following the mountain streams
I wander singing along distant paths
Or sit and watch the white clouds
Billowing from jagged peaks
Pity the traveler in the floating world
Of fame and fortune
His life spent chasing after specks of swirling dust.

Other modern scholars such as Imoto Nōichi, Kurita Isamu, and Iriya Yoshitaka conclude that Ryōkan was completely secular, or too secular, and that his spiritual insights and qualities were fleeting moments rather than an attained condition. But these scholars ignore the poems in which Ryōkan expresses supreme calm and contentment. Instead, they accent the poems that point to Ryōkan's position *within* the normal conditions in which humans live in the world. Here are some examples of his poems which support the conclusion of these scholars:

The long winter night! The long winter night seems endless;
When will it be day?
No flame in the lamp nor charcoal in the fireplace;
Lying in bed, listening to the sound of freezing rain.
To an old man, dreams come easy;
I let my thoughts drift.
The room is empty and both the *saké* [rice wine] and the oil are used up—
The long winter night.

When I was a boy studying in an empty hall,
Over and over I had to fill the lamp with oil.
Even now, that task is disagreeable—
The long winter night.

Will my stupidity and stubbornness ever end?
Poor and alone—that's my life
Twilight on the streets of a ramshackle town
Going home again with my empty bowl.

Who is there to pity this life of mine?
A pepper tree props up the brushwood gate
Mugwort obliterates the narrow garden path
On my bamboo fence dangles a solitary gourd
Across the valley
I hear the sounds of trees being felled
And spend the clear morning
with my head on the pillow
A mountain bird trills a few notes as it passes
As if trying to console me in my solitude.

I sit quietly, listening to the falling leaves—

A lonely hut, a life of renunciation.
The past has faded, things are no longer remembered.
My sleeve is wet with tears.

Light sleep, the bane of old age:
Dozing off, evening dreams, waking again.
The fire in the hearth flickers; all night a steady rain
Pours off the banana tree.
Now is the time I wish to share my feelings—
But there is no one.

However, Ryūichi Abé has sought, and found, a middle ground between these two extremes. He argues that the Buddhist notion of "non-duality" exhibited by Ryōkan holds in tandem tension the emphasis on Ryōkan's appearing unenlightened and a secular poet and the emphasis on Ryōkan's appearing enlightened and a spiritual master. "Non-duality" is the perception in Buddhism that the typical or normal things that we see as opposites, are, in fact, truly not oppositional but instead integrated but different aspects of a single reality. This means that good and evil, beauty and ugliness, youth and old age, wisdom and foolishness, masculinity and femininity, and enlightenment and non-enlightenment are not dichotomous but instead aspects of one entity. As a result, in these terms Ryōkan reflects both normal and ordinary human emotions such as loneliness, distress, hunger, disappointment, and depression; and he also exhibits enlightened qualities such as calmness, serenity, mindfulness, and non-attachment. The world of enlightenment and the world of normal human experience are not mutually exclusive, but rather interpenetrating features of a single reality.[14]

As Ryōkan puts it,

> Cling to truth and it turns into falsehood. Understand falsehood and it turns into truth. Truth and falsehood are two sides of the same coin.

14. Abé, "Poetics of Mendicancy," 27–47.

Neither accept one nor reject the other.[15]

Or,

Illusion and enlightenment? Two sides of a coin.
Universals and particulars? No difference.[16]

Reflecting this non-dual, single reality, Ryōkan, in Abé's opinion, was a *bodhisattva*. This term in Buddhism means a person who is able to reach nirvana but delays doing so out of compassion in order to save suffering beings. So, the *bodhisattva* is deliberately and intentionally caught between this world and the world of enlightenment. Ryōkan is therefore reflecting normal human experience—identifying with all of us—and at the same time presenting to us the characteristics and qualities of someone who is enlightened. We can then be drawn to his model and example and be inspired to pursue non-attachment and enlightenment.

Significant especially for our study are the implications of this non-duality for the relationship between humans and nature. Typically, Westerners consider themselves as separate from nature and distant from it. Language used in statements such as, "I will leave where I am and go for a walk out in nature," "I enjoy journeying far away to the wilderness out there," "Nature is beneath us to serve us," or "I have planned a trip that leaves my everyday life in order to explore the wonder of the natural world" points to nature as something different from us, outside of us, separate, and (to make a value judgment) less important than we are. Nature is regarded as a reality with which we have nothing to do unless we elect to go out and engage it, and nature is understood as a reality which is inferior to us and only gains its value by its worth and service to us.

For Ryōkan, nature is something of which we humans are a part. We belong to nature more than nature belongs to us. In Zen Buddhism, nothing in the universe exists independently,

---

15. As translated in Ross, *1,001 Pearls*, 36.
16. From Tanahashi, *Sky Above*, 1–45.

separated from the rest. Instead, everything is interrelated.[17] As a result, humans and (the rest of) nature are interconnected. We are inextricably a part of the natural world. And the other parts of nature have value, in and of themselves. They do not gain value by serving us; they already have value by their "being."[18]

Of course, the academic discipline of environmental science has taught this human relationship with nature for a prolonged period of time. All species are connected; all living things are strands in life's web. Evolutionary biology has also accented the same point. Mold and human beings share largely the same DNA! And chimpanzees and humans share 97 percent of the same genetic material. We humans are intimately and organically connected to the rest of life on Earth.[19]

And nature has something to say to us, if we will just overcome the "cultural autism" of which the late Thomas Berry has spoken and the "spiritual Alzheimer's" which Pope Francis has diagnosed.[20]

(Untitled)
The rain has stopped, the clouds have drifted away,
and the weather is clear again.
If your heart is pure, then all things in your world are pure.
Abandon this fleeting world, abandon yourself,
Then the moon and flowers will guide you along the Way.

(emphasis mine)

From one point of view, nature reminds us of our impermanence and the impermanence of all things. Flowers come and go, for nothing—no thing—lasts forever. To build our lives on the

17. The Buddhist term for this interrelationship is *pratityasamutpada* or "dependent origination"—all things are what they are only in association with all else.

18. The Buddhist term for this is *sunyata*—"suchness"; see Cain, "Self-Reliant," 117–35.

19. Cain, *Down to Earth.*

20. Brown, "War against Pope Francis," 13.

erroneous presumption that they do, is folly. "Things" do not give our life everlasting meaning.

From a second point of view, nature says to us that "nature knows best." That is, nature can "guide" us as our teacher. This insight is found in the Daoism of Asia ("follow Nature's path or Way") and the Hebrew Bible of the Jewish and Christian traditions. Jeremiah 8:7 points out that "even the stork in the heavens knows its times and the turtledove, swallow, and crane observe the time of their coming, but my people do not know the ordinance of the Lord." And Isaiah 1:3 contends that "the ox knows its owner, and the donkey its master's crib; but Israel does not know, my people do not understand." "Knowing" and "not knowing" are the keys here—animals know, but humans do not. Nature is the teacher. As Old Testament scholar, Walter Brueggemann, has concluded, "God's creatures have a wisdom about how to live well and responsibly in a world governed by the creator God."[21]

But animals alone are not the only guides available to us in nature: plants, as well, can guide us and have wisdom to share. The famous naturalist, John Muir, believed that both animate and inanimate objects have something to "say" to us:

> As I long as I live, I'll hear the birds and winds and the waterfalls sing. I'll interpret the rocks and learn the language of flood and storm and avalanche. I'll make the acquaintance of the wild gardens and the glaciers and get as near to the heart of this world as I could. And so I did. I sauntered about from rock to rock, from grove to grove, from stream to stream, and whenever I met a new plant I would sit down beside it for a minute or a day, to make its acquaintance, to hear what it had to tell. I asked the boulders where they had been and whither they were going, and when night found me, there I camped. I took no more heed to save time or to make haste than did the trees of the stars. This is true freedom, a good, practical sort of immortality.[22]

21. Brueggemann, *God of All Flesh*, 13.
22. "John Muir."

This insight is also revealed in contemporary Japan nearly two centuries after Ryōkan. Female "tree doctor" Tsukamoto Konami rose to fame about twenty years ago after transplanting four 130-year-old wisteria trees to Ashikaga Flower Park. In order to adequately plan the move and then successfully carry it out, she said that she "had to 'walk in the tree's shoes' to understand its feelings." And so, she "went to the trees and stood in front of them for a long time." Her instinct was that "they could be moved"; they "told" her they could be moved.[23] If you talk to a tree, she said, it will listen. And if you listen, the tree will talk to you.[24]

Of like mind was American Nobel Prize winner for her work in corn genes, biologist Barbara McClintock (1902–1992), who indicated that she had "intimate knowledge" of her maize plants, and that she would "ask the maize plant to solve specific problems and then watch its responses."[25] Nature will instruct us, if we will only listen and pay attention.

Ryōkan also knew the danger of avarice, for avarice is unsatisfied greed: the more we want, the more we get, and then the more we still want. We can never have enough, be enough, possess enough, or store up enough. Our longing for unneeded excess is insatiable and extends to excess wealth, excess status, excess power, even excess food. Ryōkan speaks to this by addressing our "lusting after things," our behaving like "monkeys frantically grasping for the moon in the water":

"I Watch People in the World"
I watch people in the world
Throw away their lives lusting after things,
Never able to satisfy their desires,
Falling into deeper despair
And torturing themselves.
Even if they get what they want
How long will they be able to enjoy it?

23. Ryall, "Woman Arborist."
24. Ryall, "Woman Arborist."
25. Keller, *Feeling*, 197–208.

For one heavenly pleasure
They suffer ten torments of hell,
Binding themselves more firmly to the grindstone.
Such people are like monkeys
Frantically grasping for the moon in the water
And then falling into a whirlpool.
How endlessly those caught up in the floating world suffer.
Despite myself, I fret over them all night
And cannot staunch my flow of tears.[26]

Ryōkan recognizes that "things" do not, cannot, grant us immense and lasting meaning and happiness in life:

"You Do Not Need Many Things"
My house is buried in the deepest recess of the forest
Every year, ivy vines grow longer than the year before.
Undisturbed by the affairs of the world I live at ease,
Woodmen's singing rarely reaching me through the trees.
While the sun stays in the sky, I mend my torn clothes
And facing the moon, I read holy texts aloud to myself.
Let me drop a word of advice for believers of my faith.
To enjoy life's immensity, you do not need many things.[27]

And a portion of a poem quoted before:

Pity the traveler in the floating world
Of fame and fortune
His life spent chasing after specks of swirling dust.

One famous story about Ryōkan and his awareness that one does not need "things" and certainly not "many things" to find enjoyment in life is about a thief. One evening a thief visited Ryōkan's hut at the base of the mountain only to discover there was nothing to steal. Ryōkan returned and caught him. "You have come a long way to visit me," he told the prowler, "and you should not return

26. Stevens, *Dewdrops*, 69.
27. Yuasa, "You Do Not Need Many Things."

empty-handed. Please take my clothes as a gift." The thief was be-
wildered. He took the clothes and slunk away. Ryōkan sat naked,
watching the moon. "Poor fellow," he mused, "I wish I could have
given him this beautiful moon."[28]

On other such occasions of being robbed, Ryokan expressed
similar sentiments:

> A thief took the . . . futon
> from the thatch-roofed room.
> Who could blame him?
> The thief left it behind:
> the moon
> at my window.[29]

And his "way of being" in the world was characterized by
humility. Ryōkan led in large part the life of a hermit, with few,
if any, of the customary marks of success regardless of the particular cultural society we are considering. He was a societal drop-
out, living mostly as a hermit and a beggar. He liked playing with
children, perhaps even more than being with adults. He also held
few of the signs of "successful Buddhism": He never became the
head of a monastery or a temple. He had no *protégé* designed and
destined to carry on his teachings (no "*dharma* heir"—a successor to perpetuate his teaching). Similar to Saint Francis, he never
had recorded a collection of his teachings (in a sense, his life—like
Saint Francis's—*was* his teachings).

> (Untitled)
> Truly, I love this life of seclusion.
> Carrying my staff, I walk toward a friend's cottage.
> The trees in his garden, soaked by the evening rain,
> Reflect the cool, clear autumnal sky.
> The owner's dog comes to greet me;
> Chrysanthemums bloom along the fence.

---

28. Written after a thief robbed his hut, as translated in Mitchell, *Enlightened Heart*, 96–98.

29. Tanahashi, *Sky Above*, 61.

These people have the same spirit as the ancients;
An earthen wall marks their separation from the world.
In the house volumes of poetry are piled on the floor.
Abandoning worldliness, I often come to this tranquil place—
The spirit here is the spirit of Zen.[30]

Zen poetry and Zen teachings frequently put forth the theme of "abandoning the world." In this context, it means that we must forego the typical marks of success and meaning that the world suggests as the most important things in life. Wealth, power, status/popularity, comfort, and pleasure are often what the world evaluates in assessing a person's worth. As many have pointed out, "This is especially true in American culture."[31] Any person who does not pursue and achieve such "indicators of success, worth, and happiness" is a societal failure. In this sense, Ryōkan and Zen are counter-cultural, unworldly "failures."[32]

Just as the Buddha—Prince Siddhartha Gautama—turned away from the benefits of a royal family membership guaranteeing power, status, and wealth; just as Saint Francis turned away from the fortune and security and social standing of the Italian textile business he would inherit; and just as Taigu Ryōkan gave up being the "village headman-in-waiting with a future of prosperity and power": so the "worldling," then, must transform himself or herself in terms of a basic attitude toward life. This necessitates a renunciation, a repenting, a turning away from what the world and culture cherish to what one has discerned and learned is better, higher, superior, and more satisfying. Success is not found in cash but in character, not how much we have but in the way we live, not how envied our possessions are by others but rather what kind of person we are.

If someone asks what is the mark of enlightenment or illusion,
I cannot say—wealth and honor are nothing but dust,
As the evening rain falls, I sit in my hermitage

30. Chowaney, "Ryokan," para. 16.
31. Stevens, *One Robe*, 15. See also Chowaney, "Ryokan."
32. Stevens, *Dewdrops*, 69.

And stretch out both feet in answer.

The ridicule or praise of worldly people means nothing

This is an old truth; don't think it was discovered recently.

"I want this, I want that."

Is nothing but foolishness.

I'll tell you a secret:

All things are impermanent.

I have nothing to report, my friends.

If you want to find the meaning,

Stop chasing after so many things.[33]

Ryōkan's humility also expressed itself in his unwillingness to judge other persons. He embraced persons who were different, just as Saint Francis had embraced marginalized lepers in his own thirteenth-century society.

> When you encounter those who are wicked, unrighteous, foolish, dim-witted, deformed, vicious, chronically ill, lonely, unfortunate, or disabled, you should think: "How can I save them?" And even if there is nothing you can do, at least you must not indulge in feelings of arrogance, superiority, derision, scorn, or abhorrence, but should immediately manifest sympathy and compassion. If you fail to do so, you should feel ashamed and deeply reproach yourself: "How far I have strayed from the Way! How can I betray the old sages? I take these words as an admonition to myself."[34]

Ryōkan also made do with what he had. He was a master artist and calligrapher who had a very distinct style. In part, his technique of using a very thin line in his calligraphy was due to the fact that he often used twigs rather than brushes. He could not afford brushes because of his self-imposed poverty (recall that Saint Francis, too, had taken a vow of poverty and had married "Lady Poverty"). And when he had no paper, he practiced his brush strokes by waving his fingers in the air.

33. Stevens, *One Robe*, 45.
34. Meng-hu, "Zen Poetics," para. 11.

Ryōkan was also concerned about being wasteful. In a gross but insightful action described below, he stands against wasting food and also simultaneously demonstrates a concern for living things—although maggots to most of us are quite disgusting.

Any food that [Ryōkan] was offered that he did not eat, he put into a little pot. Over time, the food rotted and became filled with maggots and other bugs. When warned against eating it, all Ryōkan said was, "No, no, it's all right. I let the maggots escape before I eat it, and it tastes just fine!"

This combination of not being wasteful and respecting all life forms, regardless of their "lowliness" is captured by the Japanese term, もったいない (*mottainai*). It has roots in Shinto (a native religion/philosophy of life in Japan) and also in the Buddhism that was imported to Japan in the sixth century from China via Korea. *Mottainai* has crept into use in modern-day Japan after a hiatus due to the term's previously falling into disfavor because of its feudal and frugal original context: In an earlier age, Japan was quite poor, and people were forced to be painfully thrifty and had to scrimp to get by.[35]

Its recovery and reemphasis today are environmentally relevant because it bumps up against both "wastefulness" and "sacrilege."[36] *Mottainai* means simultaneously "don't be wasteful" and "don't be sacrilegious." In other words, because nature is sacred, and wasting resources and harming the land would be an error or a "sin" (to impose a Western term on an Eastern dynamic), out of respect and gratitude we should be frugal.

It needs to be acknowledged here that though Japanese culture may be philosophically green-attuned, it is not practically so. Although the concept and advice of *mottainai* have deep and important Japanese cultural roots, Japanese industry has been rapacious in its exploitation of resources, both inside the country and outside. Logging in countries where Japanese influence

35. Maathai, *Replenishing Earth*, 106–10.

36. Consultation with Professor of Philosophy and Religion and Department Chair Dr. James McRae, an expert on Eastern religions and philosophies, at Westminster College, July 24, 2018.

is strong—such as Malaysia—is but one example. Overfishing is a second. And, as an instance of waste production, twenty-four billion one-use chopsticks are thrown away in Japan every year.[37]

However, the hinging of gratitude (out of respect) and of responsible use of resources (avoiding wastefulness) is a suggestive and helpful plank in a platform of wise and responsible care of nature, of which we are intimately a part.

Although Ryōkan was restrained in terms of the clothes he wore and the food he ate and the things that he had in his possession, he did not always act within the restraints of being a Zen Buddhist monk. It is common practice for a monk to abstain from eating meat. Once a young monk sat to dinner with Ryōkan and watched him eat fish. When asked why, Ryōkan replied, "I eat fish when it's offered, but I also let the fleas and flies feast on me [when sleeping at night]. Neither bothers me at all." Again, here his response points to being unconventional on meat consumption but conventional in his Buddhist attitude of sensitivity, compassion, and nonviolence regarding other living things.

In a similar vein, it is said that Ryōkan only slept with most of his body inside of a mosquito net so that he would not hurt the bugs outside. At the same time, he protruded one leg from the net so that the mosquitoes would not go hungry!

And he was unconventional in that he enjoyed dancing, was fond of rice wine (sometimes drinking it to excess—"I send one of the children to buy some country wine/and after I'm drunk, toss off a few lines of calligraphy"[38]), and also attended the midsummer Bon Festivals: Bon (盆) is a Japanese Buddhist custom to honor the spirits of one's ancestors. This Buddhist-Confucian custom has evolved into a family reunion holiday during which people return to ancestral family places to visit and clean their ancestors' graves, during which the spirits of ancestors are supposed to revisit the household altars. It has been celebrated in Japan for more than five hundred years and traditionally includes a dance, known as Bon-Odori. This festival lasts for three days. Because he was a monk,

37. Maathai, *Replenishing Earth*, 108.
38. Stevens, *Three Zen Masters*, 127–28.

Ryōkan would normally be unable to attend, but regularly sneaked in disguised as a woman.

At the end of his life, this conventional/unconventional, eccentric, *bodhisattva*, mendicant monk shared these thoughts on the fleetingness of time and of his imminent demise:

> (Untitled)
>
> The sun sets, and all living things cease to stir
> I, too, close my brushwood gate
> A few crickets begin to chirp
> The color of grasses and trees has faded
> Burning stick after stick of incense
> I meditate through the long autumn night
> When my body gets cold, I put on more clothes
> Practice hard, fellow students of Zen!
> *Time is gone before you realize* [emphasis mine].[39]
>
> Life is like a dewdrop,
> Empty and fleeting;
> My years are gone
> And now, quivering and frail,
> I must fade away.

Taigu Ryōkan "faded away" on January 6, 1831, at the age of seventy-three. With him was the young nun, Teishin, with whom it appears he had fallen in love four years prior when he was sixty-nine and she was twenty-nine. Like Saint Francis so many years before with Clare at his deathbed, Teishin says that Ryōkan died as if falling asleep. Many fellow monks and farmers and nobility came to his funeral two days later to mourn his death. But his poems, his calligraphy, his memory (especially in his native Japan), and his perspective on nature all endure.

---

39. Abé and Haskel, *Great Fool*.

Recommendations for Further Reading:

Abé, Ryūichi, and Peter Haskel. *Great Fool: Zen Master Ryōkan*. Honolulu: University of Hawai'i Press, 1996.

Kownachi, Mary Lou. *Between Two Souls: Conversations with Ryōkan*. Grand Rapids: Eerdmans, 2004.

Meng-hu. "Zen Poetics of Ryokan." *Simply Haiku: A Quarterly Journal of Japanese Short Form Poetry* 4.2 (Summer 2006). http://www.simplyhaiku. com/SHv4n2/features/Meng-hu.html.

Stevens, John. *Dewdrops on a Lotus Leaf: Zen Poems of Ryōkan*. Boston: Shambhala, 1993.

———. *One Robe, One Bowl: The Zen Poetry of Ryōkan*. Boston: Weatherhill, 2014.

Tanahashi, Kazuaki. *Sky Above, Great Wind: The Life and Poetry of Zen Master Ryokan*. Boulder: Shambhala, 2012.

Watson, Burton. *Ryōkan: Zen Monk, Poet of Japan*. New York: Columbia University Press, 1977.

Yuasa, Nobuyuki. *The Zen Poems of Ryōkan*. Princeton: Princeton University Press, 1981.

Chapter Four

POPE FRANCIS

The Pontiff of the Poor and for Nature

AS HUMAN BEINGS, WE are often resistant to change. We grow accustomed to certain situations, patterns, and traditions. What's familiar is comforting to us and predictable for us.

But the case can be made that we human beings also need to grow. In fact, human beings historically have been very adaptable. This adaptability has made possible our biological survival as a species. From an evolutionary point of view, if we cease to adapt, we prepare to die.

From a theological point of view, if we cease to adapt, we succumb to irrelevance. How is an ancient religion like Christianity from two thousand years ago to be applied to the lived realities and challenges we face today? But, on the other hand, if we too easily change, or change too much, we risk giving up too much and thereby losing the treasure we have inherited, the spiritual wisdom of the ages that has been passed down to us.

Therefore, there is a necessary, and potentially creative, tension between our rootedness to the wisdom of the past (the tradition teaches the world) and our openness to innovation in the present (the world teaches the tradition). And whether one is religious in a Christian way (or specifically a Roman Catholic way or a

Protestant or Eastern Orthodox way), religious in a non-Christian way, or not religious at all, our approach toward the papacy of the Catholic Church may evaluate its current state as being too fixed to the past or too adaptive to the present world.

Francis is a pope with both introversion to preservation and extroversion to change. In a number of ways, he is quite traditional and intends to preserve the historical and theological legacy which has been granted to him in his role as the spiritual head of over one billion Roman Catholics around the world. His stance on abortion, for example, links him to a prevalent and historic position in the Roman Catholic Church. At the same time, in a number of ways, he is quite open to change and is willing to consider making adjustments in the teachings and recommendations of the faith. His position on the side of immigrants and his unbridled criticism of capitalism—as well as his consideration of giving communion to divorced and remarried Catholics and his strong advocacy for working to halt climate change—are pushing the envelope for innovation in the teachings and recommendations of the faith.

Regardless of whether Pope Francis is loved or loathed (and he is both) as such an agent for change, he has brought new clerical characteristics (he represents a number of "firsts"), a freshness of thought, and a modesty and humility of bearing to his role as pontiff.

Born in Argentina as Jorge Mario Bergoglio on December 17, 1936, in a Buenos Aires neighborhood, Pope Francis is the 266th pontiff—the first from the Americas, the first from the southern hemisphere, and the first from the Jesuit order. While the archbishop of Buenos Aires from 1998–2011 (resigning according to canon law at the age of seventy-five) and a cardinal for fifteen years, he distinguished himself by his identification with the poor. In solidarity with residents eking out an existence in the face of steep economic challenges, he lived in modest housing, used public transportation (traveling extensively throughout the diocese on the underground and on buses as opposed to private car), and doubled the number of priests serving the Buenos Aires slums. He was widely-known in his home country as the "slum bishop."

Both of his parents were linked to immigrants: his father migrating from northern Italy to escape the fascism of Benito Mussolini and the oppression of the Blackshirts, and his mother, born in Argentina, of immigrants also from the northern part of Italy in the Piedmontese-Genoese region. During this time, a large number of Italians emigrated from Italy to Argentina, and beyond the political impetus to escape Italy, there were economic advantages as well since the *per capita* income was higher in Argentina than in any European country. His father, Mario, worked as an accountant for an Argentinian railway, and his mother, Regina Maria Sivori, embraced domestically the rearing of their five children, of whom Pope Francis was the eldest. He and his sister, Maria Elena, are the current surviving siblings.[1]

A strong supporter of Argentinian soccer (*futbal*)—especially the local Buenos Aires team, "San Lorenzo"—he also loves the music of the tango and as a young man was romantically inclined to a similarly-aged woman, Amalia Damonte, who shared this interest.[2] He surprised admirers when he revealed in an interview that he had once served as the bouncer at a Buenos Aires nightclub. After focusing on chemistry in vocational/technical secondary school, he first worked in a food lab. Then he discerned a call to ministry and in 1958 became a novice in the Society of Jesus (Jesuits). He graduated with a degree in philosophy in 1963 from the Colegio de San José in San Miguel and was a seminarian from 1967–69 at the same institution. He was ordained in 1969, and later served from 1980–86 as rector and professor of theology at his *alma mater*. This was followed by finishing his doctorate in Germany, where he graduated from Freiburg in 1986.

As a result of his ethnic background and his professional experience, he is fluent in a number of languages, among them his native Spanish, Latin (the official language of the Vatican), Italian (the everyday language of the Vatican City), German, English, and Portuguese. He learned the English language through an intensive program in Dublin, Ireland, during the first three months of 1980.

1. Allen, *Miracle of Francis*.
2. Cool, *Francis*, 77.

Pope Francis was elected pontiff on March 13, 2013. He is the first non-European pope elected since the year 741, when Gregory III from Syria became pope. He chose the name Francis in honor of Saint Francis of Assisi, after his friend, Cardinal Claudio Hummes, approached him following his election and whispered to him, "Don't forget the poor." This gesture brought to his mind the thirteenth-century Saint Francis, a person who, as we have noted, had embraced poverty as the defining characteristic of his life.

It is revealing of his character and humility to note that eight years before, as Cardinal Bergoglio, he participated in the conclave in which Pope Benedict XVI was elected. It is well-known that he was the runner-up in this election. In fact, according to an anonymous cardinal's notebook, Bergoglio made a humble and passionate, emotional appeal to the other cardinals not to vote for him for he was anxious that the tight race between himself and Joseph Ratzinger (Pope Benedict XVI) could and would delay the election of the new pope.

This kind of humility has directed the tone of his papacy. Examples of his humble approach to things which the media have exposed after his election have been the fact that he returned to the boarding house where he had been staying to pay his bill personally, rather than send an assistant, and that he would choose to live in a simple two-room apartment (the *Domus Sanctae Marthae* guesthouse) rather than the traditional and luxurious papal accommodations in the Vatican's Apostolic Palace used by his predecessors. "My people are poor and I am one of them," he said in explaining his decision to live in an apartment and cook his own supper.

But he had lived a humble life personally and professionally beforehand: When John Paul II designated him a cardinal, assigning him the title of "San Roberto Bellarmino," he asked followers and friends not to come to Rome to celebrate his elevation to cardinal, but rather to donate to the poor what they would have spent on the journey.

Eight months after his election as Pope, he was named the Person of the Year in the December 2013 issue of *Time* magazine.

His tenure has been characterized by "humility and outspoken support of the world's poor and marginalized people, and he has been involved actively in areas of political diplomacy and environmental advocacy."[3]

This environmental advocacy became incarnate in literary form in his papal encyclical, *Laudato 'Si*, which was issued on May 15, 2015. In fact, Pope Francis's encyclical on climate change presents an important message to the 1.2 billion Catholic Christians worldwide and, by extrapolation, to Protestant Christians and Orthodox Christians as well: Global climate change is a religious, moral issue, the Pope contends, and it is imperative that humans respond to it in ways that demonstrate to God that they are starting to take better care of the creation that God has placed so trustingly into their hands.

> A very solid scientific consensus indicates that we are presently witnessing a disturbing warming of the climatic system. In recent decades, this warming has been accompanied by a constant rise in the sea level and, it would appear, by an increase of extreme weather events, even if a scientifically determinable cause cannot be assigned to each particular phenomenon. Humanity is called to recognize the need for changes of lifestyle, production and consumption, in order to combat this warming or at least the human causes which produce or aggravate it.[4]

The late Pope John Paul II had pointed in 1979 to Saint Francis as the patron saint of ecology, and Pope Francis, as has been previously noted, took his pontifical name from this patron saint. In fact, the encyclical *Laudato Si'* borrows its title from a canticle of Saint Francis, *Laudato Si', mi' Signore* ("Praise be to you, my Lord"). This canticle regards nature as an intimate subject to which we humans are deeply related. In fact, our praise is to be given to God through our "Sister, Mother Earth."

3. "Pope Francis Biography," para. 1.

4. Francis, *Laudato Si'*, paras. 23, 20; for more on global warming and climate change, see paras. 24–26, 52, 169–70, 172, 175, 181, and 188.

> Praise be to you, my Lord, through our Sister, Mother
> Earth, who sustains and governs us, and who produces
> various fruit with colored flowers and herbs.[5]

Pope Francis's thought and writing indicate a similar perspective on the natural world:

> I do not want to write this Encyclical without turning to
> that attractive and compelling figure, whose name I took
> as my guide and inspiration when I was elected Bishop of
> Rome. I believe that Saint Francis is the example *par excellence* of care for the vulnerable and of an integral ecology lived out joyfully and authentically. He is the patron
> saint of all who study and work in the area of ecology,
> and he is also much loved by non-Christians . . . [He]
> lived in simplicity and in wonderful harmony with God,
> with others, with nature, and with himself. He shows us
> just how inseparable the bond is between concern for
> nature, justice for the poor, commitment to society, and
> interior peace.[6]

The subtitle of this second encyclical from Pope Francis—*On Care for Our Common Home*—directs the reader to several points. First, humans are in this together—there are no boundaries and exemptions in environmental issues; instead, they are transnational in character and scope. Indeed, as author Daniel Quinn points out in his best-selling book, *Ishmael*,[7] no one, no people, no species, is exempt from natural laws, from the cycles and rhythms of nature. Just as no animate or inanimate object is unaffected by the law of gravity, for example, no animate or inanimate object is invulnerable to environmental issues. The exposure may vary, and the impact may be greater or lesser, but damage to nature impacts everything, everyone, everywhere.

Second, our historical penchant for regarding ourselves as the lords and masters of nature is not only presumptuous but has

---

5. Saint Francis, "Canticle of Creatures," 113–14.

6. Francis, *Laudato Si'*, paras. 10, 11–12; there is more on Francis of Assisi on 12–13.

7. Quinn, *Ishmael*.

contributed to the plundering and defaming of nature. Our homocentric (human-centered) attitude has led to the depletion (or threatened depletion) of natural resources and to the poisoning of air, land, and water. Pope Francis concludes that the earth "is among the most abandoned and maltreated of our poor."[8]

It is significant that he sees nature's plundering as the symptom of this attitudinal disease. If/since we humans believe that the earth "belongs" to us, we then conclude that we can do anything we want to it. And we *have*: From species extinction to CO_2 emissions to garbage generation (what His Holiness calls "the throwaway society") to climate change, we have interfered with nature's capacity to provide, self-cleanse, and regenerate.

His Eastern Christian counterpart, Patriarch Bartholomew, preceded the Pope in calling attention to this: Widely termed the "Green Patriarch," Bartholomew admonished Orthodox Christians for their role in harming the planet, calling them to acknowledge their (by extrapolation, "our") "contribution . . . to the disfigurement and destruction of creation."[9]

> For human beings to destroy the biological diversity of God's creation; for human beings to degrade the integrity of the earth by causing changes in its climate; by stripping the earth of its natural forests or destroying its wetlands; for human beings to contaminate the earth's waters, its land, its air, and its life—these are sins.[10]

Patriarch Bartholomew shared these words over twenty years ago.

In general terms, so have previous Roman Catholic popes: Pope Paul VI referred in 1971 (forty-eight years ago) to the exploitation of nature with the warning that we threaten our own survival as a species when we jeopardize the survival of Earth's natural systems—we become a "victim of [the] degradation" we have caused. He added that, obviously, there is a very "urgent need

8. Francis, *Laudato Si'*, para. 2.
9. Francis, *Laudato Si'*, para. 8.
10. Francis, *Laudato Si'*, para. 8; see Chryssavgis, *On Earth*.

for a radical change" in human conduct in our relationship with nature.[11]

Pope John Paul II (pontiff from 1978–2005), in his first encyclical in 1979, criticized our regard for the natural world as valuable only for our "immediate use and consumption."[12] Twenty-two years later, he would call for a global "ecological conversion" in the way in which we see nature.[13]

Benedict XVI, known in some Catholic circles as the "green pope," directed a number of statements throughout his pontificate (2005–2013) toward the environment. In his "Address to Students" on November 28, 2011, he said, "Friar Francis, faithful to Sacred Scripture, invites us to recognize nature as a stupendous book, [one] that speaks to us of God, of his beauty and of his goodness."[14] Pope Francis would later add in a speech to university youth in Manila, the Philippines that "a second key area where you are called to make a contribution is in showing concern for the environment. This is not only because this country, more than many others, is likely to be seriously affected by climate change. More than this, you are called to care for creation not just as responsible citizens, but also as followers of Christ!"[15]

Benedict XVI, in an "Address to Reichstag" on September 22, 2011, admonished,

> I would say that the emergence of the ecological movement in German politics since the 1970s, while it has not exactly flung open the windows, nevertheless was and continues to be a cry for fresh air which must not be ignored or pushed aside, just because too much of it is seen to be irrational. Young people have come to realize that something is wrong in our relationship with nature, that matter is not just raw material for us to shape at will, but that the earth has a dignity of its own and that we

11. Paul, *Octogesima Adveniens*.

12. John Paul, *Redemptor Hominis*.

13. John Paul, *Catechesis* (January 17, 2001), para. 4.

14. Benedict XVI, "Address of His Holiness," para. 7.

15. Francis, "Meeting with Young People," para. 30.

must follow its directives. In saying this, I am clearly
not promoting any particular political party—nothing
could be further from my mind. If something is wrong
in our relationship with reality, then we must all reflect
seriously on the whole situation and we are all prompted
to question the very foundations of our culture. Allow
me to dwell a little longer on this point. The importance
of ecology is no longer disputed. We must listen to the
language of nature and we must answer accordingly.[16]

Pope Francis, then, is not creating a precedent, he is following
one (though with an enlarged and heightened accent). But in this
encyclical, he deliberately and explicitly combines science with
theology. In fact, he devotes an entire section of *Laudato Si'* to an
analysis by science of our environmental challenges. He begins
by noting "rapidification," which refers to the speed with which
technology and human activity are catapulting us into an inten-
sification of the pace of life and work. His Holiness contrasts this
breakneck speed with the comparatively slow pace of biological
evolution. He indicates that the goals of this rapid change do not
always further the common good, but more often cause harm to
life and its quality. He appreciates the more critical perspective on
progress that has been developing recently and eroding an uncriti-
cal, "irrational confidence in progress and human abilities."[17]

Procedurally, Pope Francis discusses our environmental
problems, and then taps our spiritual resources. Although he is
speaking especially to Roman Catholic Christians—who are the
sheep of his particular flock—he is also appealing to other flocks of
sheep with different shepherds (Protestant Christians and Eastern
Orthodox Christians) and to different flocks (other religions and
also people of good will who are not necessarily religious but who
are concerned/who need to be concerned with this issue).

He begins his discussion of the present aspects of our environmental challenges by addressing pollution and climate change.
Pope Francis addresses the various forms of toxification of the

16. Benedict, "Visit to the Federal Parliament," para. 9.
17. Francis, *Laudato Si'*, paras. 18, 19.

atmosphere, land, and waters of the earth. He is quick to point out that the humans most affected negatively by this poisoning of the planet are the poor. He also laments the disposable waste debacle created by a "throwaway culture": "The earth, our home, is beginning to look more and more like an immense pile of filth."[18]

He also affirms climate change as real (not a "hoax"): "A very solid scientific consensus indicates that we are presently witnessing a disturbing warming of the climatic system."[19] He then goes on to indict humans for climate change, saying it is primarily caused by human activity (not as simply and only the result of a natural pattern or rhythm of Earth's atmospheric fluctuation). Most global warming in recent decades is due to the great concentration of greenhouse gases, released mainly as a result of human activity.[20] In this, he sides with the majority (over 95 percent) of the world's scientists and the IPCC (Intergovernmental Panel on Climate Change). As a result, he calls upon humans to make changes in their lifestyle, consumption, and production; specifically, he recognizes and criticizes our heavy reliance upon fossil fuels as lying at the heart of the problem. He then points out the repercussions of climate change, ranging from rising sea levels to loss of biodiversity, and especially points out the plight of the poor in the face of these consequences.

Concerning the issue of available and potable water, he discusses this in the context of the depletion of natural resources. Because water is crucial to human life and to the health of ecosystems, and because the earth's poor have limited access to safe drinking water, he asserts that "access to safe drinkable water is a basic and universal human right."[21]

Alarmed also by biodiversity loss, Pope Francis insists that the reduction of forests and woodlands, resulting in the loss of species which are resources for food and for curing disease, is not a matter solely of extrinsic value but also of intrinsic value. That

18. Francis, *Laudato Si'*, paras. 21, 22.
19. Francis, *Laudato Si'*, paras. 23.
20. Francis, *Laudato Si'*, para. 23.
21. Francis, *Laudato Si'*, para. 30.

is, these losses are not negative and regrettable simply because we humans suffer as a result, but also because these species "have value in themselves."[22] Since "the great majority become extinct for reasons related to human activity,"[23] humans bear the blame for this situation.

Pope Francis goes on to reflect theologically that "thousands of species will no longer give glory to God by their very existence, nor convey their message to us."[24] In this lamentation, he echoes Saint Francis, who believed that the natural world praised God for God's goodness and God's beauty. For this reason, Saint Francis preached to the animals—especially the birds—and called upon them to proclaim the presence and the power of the Creator, along with humans, giving gratitude to God for their existence. In addition, the Pope also echoes the Hebrew Bible of the Jewish tradition and the Qur'an of the Muslim tradition. In *Tanach* (the Jewish Scriptures), the hills, the trees, aquatic creatures, wild and domesticated animals, birds, and crawling insects all shout forth with joy at their Creator's handiwork in creating them and all creation:

> The mountains and the hills before you shall burst into song, and all the trees of the field shall clap their hands.[25]
>
> Praise the Lord from the earth, you sea monsters and all deeps . . .
>
> Mountains and all hills, fruits trees and all cedars! Wild animals and all cattle, creeping things and flying birds.[26]
>
> Then shall the trees of the forest sing for joy before the Lord . . .[27]
>
> Let the heavens be glad, and let the earth rejoice; let the sea roar, and all that fills it; let the field exult, and everything in

---

22. Francis, *Laudato Si'*, paras. 33, 140.

23. Francis, *Laudato Si'*, para. 33.

24. Francis, *Laudato Si'*, para. 33.

25. Ps 55:12b.

26. Ps 148:7, 9–10.

27. 1 Chr 16:33a.

it. Then shall all the trees of the forest sing for joy before the Lord . . .[28]

In the *ayats* (verses) of the *Qur'an*, there is an appreciation for the *ayats* (signs) of God's creative "hand" in the universe. Indeed, in Islam there is the sense that nature reveals the existence, power, and goodness of *Allah* (God) no less than the revelation contained in the *Qur'an*. The use of the same word (*ayats*) makes the point clear in Islamic theology.

> Everything in the heavens and on earth glorifies God.[29]
>
> The seven heavens and the earth and all they contain glorify God, and there is not a thing but extols his glory . . .[30]
>
> O you hills and birds, echo his psalms of praise.[31]
>
> Do you not see that all things that are in the heavens and on earth bow down in worship to God—the sun, the moon, the stars, the hills, the trees, the animals, and a great number of human beings?[32]

Returning to the Pope's point that all creatures have intrinsic value, this means that "each must be cherished with love and respect, for all of us as living creatures are dependent on one another." That is, each organism has intrinsic value independent of its usefulness (extrinsic value): "Each organism, as a creature of God, is good and admirable in itself."[33]

This arena of ethical consideration and moral concern widens our normal, homocentric (human-centered) frame of reference. For most of Christian history, the tradition has been concerned, and rightly so, with the state of relations among humans. In fact, the prophets of old (e.g., Amos, Hosea, Isaiah, Jeremiah, and Micah) and of new (e.g., Martin Luther King Jr.) railed forth in criticism of the marginalization of the economically disadvantaged

28. Ps 96:11–13a.
29. Qur'an 62:1 (chapter [*sura*] 62; verse [*ayat*] 1).
30. Qur'an 17:44.
31. Qur'an 34:10.
32. Qur'an 22:18.
33. Francis, *Laudato Si'*, para. 140.

(the poor), the vulnerable (the widowed), and the defenseless (the orphaned). Prophets have criticized the exploitation of the poor by the wealthy, the powerless by the powerful, and the minority by the majority.

A lesser emphasis has been on the state of relations between humans and non-human creatures. And yet that emphasis is consistent and persistent in the Christian Bible, when one removes one's homocentric glasses and sees the fullness of scriptural texts. For example, the Sabbath day, when work is to be suspended for rest and renewal, applies to animals as well as to humans. The sabbatical affects not only humans (e.g., letting slaves go free so that indentured servitude was not without relief) but also nature (e.g., letting the fields remain fallow every seventh year so that agriculture might be relieved of production and remain sustainable). The covenant with Noah after the great flood (Gen 9) and symbolized by the rainbow applies to non-human living creatures (vv. 9–10, 12, 15–17) as well as to humans. In effect, the covenant is established (reestablished) between God and all creation, not just with humans.

Here, Pope Francis is appealing to humans (reminding humans) that our angle of moral vision is too narrow. Our camera lens is "telephoto" (focusing on humans) rather than "wide-angle" (focusing on all of life). Since God is concerned with the quality of life in all living things, and since the Bible points to such a concern, we *Homo sapiens* also ought to be so concerned.

A couple decades ago, a shift began in the realm of ethics in general and environmental ethics in particular and has continued to gain momentum and strength. "Animal rights" has become a topic of deliberation and debate.[34] And questions such as these have resulted: Do creatures have the right to exist, since they have intrinsic value? This has direct implications for the phenomenon and issue of species extinction. Are there gradations of value? Do more sentient (more conscious) creatures have a greater intrinsic

---

34. See Linzey, *Christianity and Rights*; Linzey, *Animal Theology*; Linzey, *Animal Gospel*; Linzey, *Why Animal Suffering*; Greenway, *For the Love of All Creatures*; Greenway, *Agape Ethics*; McDaniel, *Of God*; McDaniel, *Good News*.

worth, while less sentient (less conscious) creatures have lesser value? Would a cancer cell have less intrinsic value because it is a pathogen? Do creatures have the right to satisfaction even though some of them are destined to be food on our plates? And in light of animal suffering (and the alternative of our gaining protein from sources other than meat), should vegetarianism be a preferred moral ideal, if not the incumbent obligation?

Pope Francis's thought reflects the widening of ethical concern to a "biocentric ethic," to *biophilia* ("a simple love for all things, experienced as brothers and sisters").[35] Harvard biology professor emeritus E. O. Wilson, in his book of the same name (*Biophilia*), argues in an autobiographical way that we humans have "a natural affinity for life," a love of nature that is an "innate tendency" within us "to function on life processes."[36]

It should be stated that, though the Pope is definitely concerned about animal rights, he is even more concerned about the impact that environmental degradation has on us humans. He believes that forces associated with this deterioration not only erode health and meaning in human life, but also place barriers in the way of humans "[living] wisely, [thinking] deeply, and [loving] generously."[37] Thus, in his view, the deterioration of the natural environment and the deterioration of the human environment are interconnected: They occur in tandem. "We cannot adequately combat environmental degradation unless we attend to causes related to human and social degradation."[38]

So, we must pay attention to the plight of the environment and to the plight of the poor. "A true ecological approach *always* becomes a social approach; it must integrate questions of justice in debates on the environment, so as to hear *both the cry of the earth and the cry of the poor*."[39] Disproportionate use of natural resources, extreme consumerism, global warming produced by

35. Boff, *Prayer*, 1.

36. Wilson, *Biophilia*, 4.

37. Francis, *Laudato Si'*, para. 47.

38. Francis, *Laudato Si'*, para. 48.

39. Francis, *Laudato Si'*, para. 49.

huge consumption on the part of some wealthy nations, export of solid and toxic waste to developing countries, pollution produced in developing countries by companies whose standards are drastically reduced in those contexts, and foreign debt of poor countries all impact the poor of the world.

Pope Francis is also deeply concerned about what he terms "weak responses" to this: Despite the enormity of the issues and the urgency with which they challenge us, we have "never . . . hurt and mistreated our common home as we have in the last two hundred years."[40] "The problem is that we still lack the culture needed to confront the crisis."[41]

Consequently, we suffer from incapable leadership, a lack of a legal framework which can set boundaries, failure of global summits, "superficial rhetoric, sporadic acts of philanthropy, and perfunctory expressions of concern for the environment."[42] As a result, "as often occurs in periods of deep crisis which require bold decisions, we are tempted to think that what is happening is not entirely clear . . . Such evasiveness serves as a license to carrying on with our present lifestyles and models of production and consumption."[43]

Having analyzed the environmental problems—including poverty—that beset and challenge us, he then taps principles from the Judeo-Christian tradition which make mandatory our commitment to the environment. The Pope argues for the importance and necessity of both science and religion to address and correct environmental issues. "Given the complexity of the ecological crisis and its multiple causes, we need to realize that the solutions will not emerge from just one way of interpreting and transforming reality."[44] "Faith convictions can offer Christians, and some other

40. Francis, *Laudato Si'*, para. 53.
41. Francis, *Laudato Si'*, para. 53.
42. Francis, *Laudato Si'*, para. 54.
43. Francis, *Laudato Si'*, para. 59.
44. Francis, *Laudato Si'*, para. 63.

believers as well, ample motivation to care for nature and for the most vulnerable of their brothers and sisters."[45]

He argues that the creation accounts in the book of Genesis declare that human beings have three fundamental, foundational relationships—to God, to one another, and to the earth. These three intertwined relationships have been ruptured: Christians call this "sin." By refusing to recognize our creaturely limitations—and by presumptuously believing and acting as if we were God—the harmony in these three relationships has been ruptured. Particularly in terms of nature, the harmony that Saint Francis felt with all other creatures has been lost.

This disharmony, manifested in a domineering attitude and exploitative actions, is not what God-given "dominion" means, according to Pope Francis. Genesis 1:28 ("having dominion") does not grant humans license to dominate the creation and lord it over the other creatures. Instead, humans are to "till" and "tend" (serve and protect) the creation. "The Bible has no place for a tyrannical anthropocentrism [human-centeredness] unconcerned for other creatures."[46] In fact, the earth does not belong to humanity; rather, it belongs to God (Ps 24:1). Therefore, humans are not in a position to treat the earth as their possession and however they please. Instead, the earth is God's, and must be treated in ways commensurate with God's direction.

Since God views humans and other non-human living beings as having worth in themselves (intrinsic value), humans cannot view each other and other creatures as only having worth in what they contribute (extrinsic value). "Other creatures have the priority of *being* over that of *being useful.*"[47] Therefore, "the Church does not simply state that other creatures are completely subordinated to the good of human beings, as if they have no worth in themselves and can be treated as we wish."[48] "Each creature possesses its own particular goodness and perfection . . . Each of the various

45. Francis, *Laudato Si'*, para. 64.

46. Francis, *Laudato Si'*, para. 68.

47. Francis, *Laudato Si'*, para. 69.

48. Francis, *Laudato Si'*, para. 69.

creatures, willed in its own being, reflects in its own way a ray of
God's infinite wisdom and goodness. Man must therefore respect
the particular goodness of every creature, to avoid any disordered
use of things."[49]

So, again, the Sabbath day of rest involves not only humans
but also the land, the biotic community (see Gen 2:2–3; Exod
16:23; 20:10). The sabbatical year brings relief to the land after six
years of use (see Lev 25:1–6). The Jubilee Year—the fiftieth year
following seven cycles of seven years—affects both human and
non-human life (see Lev 25:10).

Beyond this, the ecological has a connection with those who
are "on the bottom" or "on the edge"—some of the harvest should
be left for the poor and the foreigners (see Lev 19:9–10). Persistent
in both the Bible and in Pope Francis's thought, there is a social
dimension to ecological sustainability.[50]

Why all these directives? The Pope says because the land/
gift of the earth/earth's fruits belongs to everyone. Of course,
ultimately, they are not even ours, but belong to God! "The created things of this world are not free of ownership."[51] But they
are not owned by us humans; instead, they belong to God. God is
the owner (see Ps 24:1; Wis 11:26—"They are yours, O Lord, who
loves the living").

Since God is the ultimate "owner" and God has created all
that is, humans *and* all other creatures are to praise God the Creator. Psalm 136:6 calls human creatures to this, and Psalm 148:3–5
calls all creatures to it—

> Praise God, sun and moon, praise God, all you shining stars!
> Praise God, you highest heavens, and you waters above the
> heavens!
> Let them praise the name of the Lord, for God commanded and
> they were created.

49. *Catechism*, part 1, sec. 2, chapter 1, art. 1, para. 5, item 339.
50. Francis, *Laudato Si'*, para. 71.
51. Francis, *Laudato Si'*, para. 89.

In fact, as the Pope reminds us by quoting Wisdom 11:24, God loves every creature in the whole world (see John 3:16).

In short, then, God has entrusted to human care a fragile human world.[52] We do not own it, but we are responsible for its welfare.[53] Consequently, the Pope contends that God seeks to draw us into the act of cooperation with the Creator.[54] Our role ought to be of "a cooperator with God in the work of creation."[55]

Pope Francis keeps within the traditional understanding of human uniqueness found in Christianity. He believes that, though we are interconnected with and related to all other species, we cannot overlook or denigrate the dignity and unique status of human beings. "All living beings [may not be put] on the same level [for that would] deprive human beings of their unique worth and the tremendous responsibility it entails."[56] The distinctiveness of humans lies in "our capacity to reason, to develop arguments, to be inventive, to interpret reality and to create art, along with other not yet discovered capacities."[57] Yet it would be mistaken to view other living beings as merely objects.[58]

The Pope's point is well-taken. Though humans share much with other living things—and are biologically and ecologically connected—humans have a distinctive and certain uniqueness. Of course, traditionally, biblically, and theologically, humans are different creatures from the other creatures because they are uniquely made in the image of God. In Genesis 1, all of life—save

---

52. Francis, *Laudato Si'*, para. 78.

53. See "In Memoriam," paras. 11–13: "We still talk in terms of conquest . . . But man is a part of nature, and his war against nature is inevitably a war against himself . . . I truly believe, that we . . . must come to terms with nature, and I think we're challenged as mankind has never been challenged before to prove our maturity and our mastery, not of nature, but of ourselves."

54. Francis, *Laudato Si'*, para. 80.

55. Francis, *Laudato Si'*, para. 117; see Hefner's notion of humans as "creative co-creators" in *Human Factor*, 7, 27, 31–32; see *Catechism*, part 1, sec. 2, chapter 1, art. 1, para. 4, item 310.

56. Francis, *Laudato Si'*, para. 90.

57. Francis, *Laudato Si'*, para. 81.

58. Francis, *Laudato Si'*, para. 82.

humans—is created by God, and though it is pronounced "good," it does not enjoy what appears to be a special status made "in the image of God."

This special status has been often understood as possessing a "soul." And "soul" has been dominantly interpreted in Greek (Platonic) ways: Humans are a combination of an earthly body and a heavenly soul, a perishable physical form containing or entrapping an imperishable spiritual component. When one dies, only the body disintegrates; the soul remains eternal.

However widespread, this interpretation is not justified by the actual meaning of the Hebrew word *nefesh* in the book of Genesis. When God breathes the breath of life into man ('*adam*), man does not suddenly now possess a "soul," rather man becomes a "living soul." In the Hebraic way of thinking, the physical dimension of a human's life and the spiritual dimension of a human's life are not two separate and independent entities. Instead, they are dimensions of a single entity, a combined reality. In this sense, a person does not *have* a soul; a person *is* a soul, a psychosomatic unity with various dimensions, among them a physical aspect and a spiritual aspect.

The relationship between body and soul as a single entity—a reality of two dimensions and not two single-dimensioned realities—may be likened to that between Kool-Aid and water. When Kool-Aid is stirred into combination with water, the two are indistinguishable. The Kool-Aid has mixed with the water, and the water has so permeated the Kool-Aid that the two are one. So, it is with the soulful aspect of a person and the physical aspect of that same person. The two dimensions are not utterly opposed to each other—like oil and water—but rather the two dimensions are intertwined, mixed, in an interconnected, unitary "whole."

French biblical scholar Oscar Cullmann, in his groundbreaking work *Immortality of the Soul or Resurrection of the Dead?*, proposes that the belief in the immortality of the soul is not Christian but pagan, not Hebrew but Greek, not contained in the Hebrew Bible/Old Testament book of Genesis but in the philosophy of

Plato.[59] Indeed, Platonic philosophy dominated the Hellenistic world and deeply influenced the thought and writings of the early fathers of the fledgling Christian Church.

Utilizing the dominant way of thinking that characterized the first five centuries of the church, these influential fathers wrote about the soul as that feature of human beings that survived the body and granted human beings a uniqueness from, and superiority over, other living things. In their eyes, in their minds, and in their writings, this constituted or specified precisely and definitively what it meant for humans to be made distinctly and distinctively "in God's image."

In their defense, one must concede the prevalence of the Platonic Greek worldview. It was, indeed, simply *the* way, or at least the *dominant* way, of understanding the world in the first half-millennium of the Christian Church. As a result, the Scriptures in general were interpreted and Christian doctrine in particular was constructed with this ever-present philosophical background in mind.

Nevertheless, it has been noted that the earliest, if not one of the oldest, Christian confessions of faith—the Apostles' Creed—does not contain as an article of faith a belief in the immortality of the soul but rather a belief in the resurrection of the body. That is, one dies as a complete entity, and one is resurrected as a complete entity.

> I believe in God the Father Almighty, maker of heaven and earth; and in Jesus Christ, his only Son, our Lord: who was conceived by the Holy Spirit, born of the virgin Mary, suffered under Pontius Pilate, was crucified, dead and buried; he descended into hell; the third day he rose again from dead; he ascended into heaven, and sits at the right hand of God the Father Almighty; from there he shall come to judge the living and the dead. I believe in the Holy Spirit, the holy catholic church, the communion of saints, the forgiveness of sins, *the resurrection of the body*, and the life everlasting. AMEN.

59. Cullmann, *Immortality.*

As Pope Francis notes, Jesus avoided any dualism.[60] He did not embrace any philosophies which demoted the physical, which then, in turn, denigrated nature. Therefore, though Platonic dualism (i.e., the physical and the spiritual, the body and the soul are utterly and completely opposed to each other) was utilized by the early church and has persisted to our time, it is not justified by the testimony of Scripture and the person of Jesus.

Of course, recognizing the accuracy of Cullmann's thesis regarding the "soul," more contemporary theologians have altered the interpretation of "image of God." Rather than humans possessing a "piece of eternity" that no other species has, they have argued for "difference" in terms of "ontological superiority"—that is, of humans being "above" the rest of creation and different in kind from other species because of some ability that we humans possess or some characteristic that is uniquely ours.

Karl Barth, the famous Swiss theologian of the last century, suggested that we humans are unique among living species not only because we, like God, are independent and free in our choices, but also because we are related to all the other species, just as God is connected to all the creation.

From basically the same time period, theologian Paul Tillich contended that we humans are different from the other species because of our rationality. We are able to reason, to think abstract thoughts, and to contemplate larger issues such as the meaning of life and where history might be going, just as God provided the rational structure of the universe—the *Logos* (the "Word) which was "with God" and "was God" (John 1:1) and which became flesh in Jesus of Nazareth (John 1:14; 3:16). Pope Francis seems to echo Tillich's point of view in his encyclical.

Biblical scholar Walter Brueggemann understands human uniqueness in terms of power. Reflecting the mandate to "have dominion" in Genesis 1:26b, he posits that we have power over the other species, just as God has power over the whole earth. But he quickly adds that we are to rule the rest of the created order in

---

60. Francis, *Laudato Si'*, para. 98, emphasis mine.

the way that God uses God's power to rule the earth—with love, justice, and service.

Contemporary Canadian theologian, Douglas John Hall, argues that being made in God's image involves not a status, but entails a responsibility. We are to be responsible for the rest of creation, just as God is responsible for the whole of creation. In other words, humans made in God's image is not something that we *have*, it is something that we *do*. It is not a privileged position, but rather a function that we perform. In short, "image of God" is a verb.[61]

Whichever one(s) of these points of view is (are) persuasive and preferable, they must be understood not in terms of separate distinction in terms of "kind," but in terms of connectional difference in terms of "degree." For example, humans are not the only species which exercises what appears to be free choice. The higher primates exhibit actions which, to the observer, look like decisions. And humans are not the only species that appear capable of rational thought—or capable of language (dolphins and killer whales communicate, the latter over hundreds of miles). Humans are not the only species that exerts power (but we have ingenious technology that grants us incredible power: In fact, we exert influence and control over vast ecosystems and hold the life and death of the whole planet in our hands). But we are not the only species that employ technology, the tools that impact and alter nature (chimpanzees use tools, and finches use sticks to extricate a meal from a tree or a hole).

So, in light of biology, ecology, and evolution, we humans are very much connected to the rest of creation, and our distinction is—at best—a matter of degree, not kind, and may not be divorced from moral responsibility and sustainable action. Recognizing this grants us humans an accurate and proper understanding of ourselves, an understanding that prompts appropriate environmental behavior: "There cannot be an adequate ecology without an adequate anthropology."[62]

61. Hall, *Imaging God*.
62. Francis, *Laudato Si'*, para. 118.

The Pope also affirms that nature is a "continuing revelation of the Divine."[63] Alongside revelation in sacred Scripture, there is in nature "a divine manifestation in the blaze of the sun and the fall of night."[64] As a result, nature is a "second Bible," to quote Francis Bacon. And Christians have two texts which provide revelation and which may be consulted for insight, guidance, and appreciation. The Bible is God's *written* Word; nature is God's *observable* Word. One can see in the Bible God's revelatory action in history, in the faith journey of a people (Israel), and in the birth, life, ministry, death, and resurrection of a human being, Jesus of Nazareth. And one can see in nature God's revelatory action in the beauty, harmony, intricacy, and evolving complexity of natural phenomena.

Pope Francis also affirms that life is interrelated and interdependent:

> Everything is connected . . . Everything is related, and we human beings are united as brothers and sisters on a wonderful pilgrimage, woven together by the love God has for each of his creatures and which also unites us in fond affection with brother sun, sister moon, brother river, and mother earth.[65]

In so doing, he reflects the *Catechism of the Catholic Church*:

> God wills the interdependence of creatures. The sun and the moon, the cedar and the little flower, the eagle and the sparrow—the spectacle of their countless diversities and inequalities tells us that no creature is self-sufficient. Creatures exist only in dependence on each other, to complete each other, in the service of each other.[66]

---

63. Francis, *Laudato Si'*, para. 85; see Canadian Conference, "You Love All that Exists," 1.

64. Pope Francis is not unique in affirming this insight; see John Paul, *Catechesis* (August 2, 2000), para. 3; and Saint Augustine, Galileo, Francis Bacon, and also Islam—the writings of Nasr especially. In all of these, nature functions as a kind of second revelatory "text."

65. Francis, *Laudato Si'*, paras. 91–92, 63–64; see para. 117, 79.

66. *Catechism*, part 1, sec. 2, chapter 1, art. 1, para. 5, item 340.

Here the Pope shares from a theological perspective what environmental science has shared from an ecological perspective. Ecosystems are interdependent: What happens to one species affects all species. When pollution befouls a body of water, all aquatic life is impacted; and even more, life that is interconnected with that pond, lake, river, or ocean is also impacted. Life is one large community of interrelated parts. Nothing is separate from the rest.

Long before science observed this, documented it, and then put it forth as a scientific "fact," "truth," "principle," or "law," Buddhism had proclaimed it. From a Buddhist perspective, no one thing is fully itself without its connections. In Buddhism, this is called *sunyata*, or nothingness. When Buddhists declare that "nothing exists" or "there is nothing," they mean that "no thing" exists by itself. It is only itself in association with other things. Perhaps more understandably put, "no one thing exists" in and of itself. "There is not one thing"; there is, instead, a web of connection. This web of connection, of interdependence, is called in Buddhism, *pratityasamutpada*. Everything is part of the whole; no part exists apart from the whole.[67]

Importantly here, *Homo sapiens* are therefore a part of nature. We are not separate from nature; we are not above nature in some sort of ranking of life. By contrast, and as indicated in a previous chapter, in the Middle Ages there was proposed a chain of being, a hierarchy of existence. It was conceived as a pyramid with God at the top; beneath God were the angels. Lower down was humanity—Adam above Eve (thereby theologically sanctioning sexism)—followed by animals, then plants, and finally, at the bottom, rocks. This ranking of reality is at odds with both the Buddhist and scientific points of view.

Native American traditions—though quite diverse in terms of language, location, customs, and values and which precede the development of religions such as Buddhism—affirm as well the "web of life." In doing so, the image and analogy of the spider's web is used: Each of the gossamer threads of the web is what it is only

---

67. Cain, "Self-Reliant," 117–36, esp. 131–35.

in connection with the other threads. If one touches one part of the web, the whole web reverberates with the impact.

Thus, it is also with nature. When one part is abused or instead cared for, the whole community of life either is harmed or helped. Therefore, there can be no isolated action.

As a result of this interconnection, we cannot honor and reflect this community of interrelationship and interaction, this intimate sense of communion with the natural order/the creation, if our hearts lack tenderness, compassion, and concern for our fellow human beings.[68] One would also be justified and wise to add to our "fellow human beings," "our fellow living beings." But the Pope here is aware that ecological concerns cannot be divorced from social concerns especially for human justice. "It is clearly inconsistent to combat trafficking in endangered species while remaining completely indifferent to human trafficking [and] remaining unconcerned about the poor."[69] However, he then returns to a fuller frame of reference when he advocates that we can hardly consider ourselves to be fully loving if we disregard *any* aspect of reality: "Peace, justice, and the preservation of creation are three absolutely interconnected themes, which cannot be separated and treated individually without once again falling into reductionism."[70]

In addition, Pope Francis is clear to make a crucial distinction about God's "location." Nature manifests God and is also a locus of God's presence. So, God's reality and presence do not lie "beyond" nature (no deism). But God's reality is not subsumed in nature (no pantheism either): God cannot be reduced or consumed by nature, for God is transcendent as well as immanent. "There is an infinite distance between God and the things of this world, which do not possess his fullness."[71] So, God fully contains the world, but the

68. Francis, *Laudato Si'*, paras. 92.

69. Francis, *Laudato Si'*, paras. 91.

70. See Dominican Episcopal Conference, "Pastoral Letter"; quoted in Francis, *Laudato Si'*, para. 92.

71. Francis, *Laudato Si'*, para. 88.

world does not fully contain God (panentheism). God is intimate in the world but is nevertheless distinctively different from it.[72]

This imbues nature with sacredness. It is sacred not only because God created it, but also because God is present in it—not reducible to it, but immanent in it. Since God is present in creation, this means that "there is a mystical meaning to be found in a leaf, in a mountain trail, in a dewdrop, or in a poor person's face."[73]

Despite the admonitions to treat other species with respect, to care for the earth, to regard nature as the dwelling place of God ("the world as God's 'body,'" to quote theologian Sallie McFague[74]) as well as being transcendent to nature, and to see nature as a second source of divine revelation, we have the environmental problems which the Pope previously catalogued.

And for these problems, he puts the blame squarely on us humans. In the "Human Roots of the Ecological Crisis" chapter of *Laudato Si'*, he cites our excessive anthropocentrism (human-centeredness) as the cause of our environmental issues. "Modernity has been marked by an excessive anthropocentrism."[75] A "Promethean vision of mastery over the world" has been its offspring. By thinking that the world was made just for us, seizing the Genesis 1 mandate to "dominate and subdue" with no counterbalance provided by the "kinder, gentler" language of Genesis 2 to "till" (serve) and "tend" (protect); by reducing nature's value as a community of interrelated subjects to a storehouse of seemingly unlimited commodities or objects which are there for our taking

---

72. "Deism" refers to God and the world being utterly opposite, separate from one another. "Pantheism" refers to God and the world being absolutely the same, identical with one another. "Panentheism" refers to God and the world being connected, but God's reality exceeds that of the world. While deism preserves God's transcendence while sacrificing God's immanence, and pantheism preserves God's immanence while sacrificing God's transcendence, panentheism preserves both God's transcendence and immanence, sacrificing neither for the sake of the other.

73. Francis, *Laudato Si'*, para. 233; here Pope Francis references the Muslim mystic, Sufi writer Ali al-Khawas: Francis, *Laudato Si'*, endnote 159.

74. McFague, "World as God's Body," 671–73.

75. Francis, *Laudato Si'*, para. 116.

and only valuable because of what they provide and can do for *us*; by developing technology that will conquer nature and harness those resources to satisfy our wants (not needs): we have blindly and obsessively embraced the values of greed, mastery, and short-term gain.

Regarding greed, he points to "the culture of consumerism, which prioritizes short-term gain and private interest."[76] He understands compulsive consumerism to be one expression of the "techno-economic paradigm," which John Paul II termed "collective selfishness."[77] Technological power plus the desire for quick economic gain leads to oppressing and exploiting nature. As a result, there needs to be a new paradigm (a new way of looking, a lifestyle, and a spirituality) which "generates resistance to the assault of the technocratic paradigm."[78] A non-consumerist model of life would result.

Plus, greed increases when people become more self-centered.[79] What *I* want becomes the most important priority to satisfy. The Pope sees this as a kind of spiritual emptiness: "The emptier a person's heart is, the more he or she needs things to buy, own, and consume."[80]

Regarding mastery, he notes that "Contemporary man has not been trained to use power well."[81] While the modification of nature for useful purposes is a distinguishing mark of the human family and has resulted in the elimination of a number of harmful evils and the overcoming of a number of limitations, it also has a dangerous underside. It itself has caused certain evils, such as pollution, for example, and the misapplication of science to pursue evil intentions (eugenics, for example, during the rule of the Nazi regime in Germany). This is the "technological paradigm" or the

76. Francis, *Laudato Si'*, para. 184.
77. John Paul, *Message*, para. 1.
78. Francis, *Laudato Si'*, para. 111.
79. Francis, *Laudato Si'*, para. 204.
80. Francis, *Laudato Si'*, para. 204.
81. Francis, *Laudato Si'*, para. 10; see Guardini, *End*, 82.

"technocratic paradigm," and its motive is to grant "lordship over all."[82]

Regarding short-term consequences, Pope Francis contends that "where profits alone count, there can be no thinking about the rhythms of nature, its phases of decay and regeneration, or the complexity of ecosystems which may be gravely upset by human intervention."[83] For example, "as long as the clearcutting of a forest increases production, no one calculates the losses entailed in the desertification of the land, the harm done to biodiversity or the increased pollution. In a word, businesses profit by calculating and paying only a fraction of the costs involved."[84]

This short-term thinking and its craving instant gratification are part and parcel of our contemporary understanding of our relationship with nature. Our fast-food culture and drive-thru mentality press us to want it *fast* and to want it *now*. What results is an unquenchable thirst that can never be satisfied and that always wants *more*.

This obsession with speed, never having enough, and wanting what we want *now* not only damages the environment, but also reduces the inheritance we leave for the next generation. This shortsightedness means that those who follow us will receive a polluted planet with diminished resources and reduced species. The Pope is aware of this when he recognizes that "the environment is part of a logic of receptivity."[85] In other words, the gifts/fruits of the creation are on loan to each generation, which then must hand it on to the next. If we care about our descendants, we must leave an inhabitable and hospitable planet to future generations. "An integral ecology is marked by this broader vision."[86]

It is said among the Iroquois that the vision of consequences was extended to the seventh generation. That is, any action undertaken should be considered in light of its long-term repercussions.

82. Francis, *Laudato Si'*, paras. 106–8.

83. Francis, *Laudato Si'*, para. 190.

84. Francis, *Laudato Si'*, para. 195.

85. Francis, *Laudato Si'*, para. 159, 106.

86. Francis, *Laudato Si'*, para. 159, 106.

What quality of ecological life are we leaving to our children, our grandchildren, and our grandchildren's children?

Pope Francis recognizes that our present mindset with its expression in a consumerist lifestyle must be changed. Indeed, a repentance from our present way of seeing and manner of acting and a conversion to a new mindset and sustainable lifestyle are desperately needed. The Pope believes that religion can, and must, play a crucial role here, for "the majority of the world's population professes to be religious believers,"[87] and religion deals with changes in mindset, attitude, and commitment. "Christian spirituality has a precious contribution to make to the renewal of humanity,"[88] for religion affirms the reality and the possibility of *metanoia*, a change of heart.

It is precisely this mindset for which the Pope is calling. He recognizes the direct connection between the way one "sees" and the actions one undertakes: One's specific perspective sanctions particular behaviors and prohibits others. Simply put, "certain mindsets influence our behavior."[89] But unfortunately, our current mindset is one of exploitation and domination; "unless we propose a new paradigm for how we understand ourselves and how we must relate to nature, the paradigm of consumerism will continue unabated."[90]

The new paradigm is one of protection and service—it is a healthy and sustainable mindset that includes gratitude that the earth is God's good gift, recognition that we are to imitate God's generosity toward the earth, and awareness that we are not disconnected from other living things but rather are bonded to all of life. In that way, he argues, we are not prompted to domination, but called to responsibility.[91] We are to embody "a culture of care."[92]

87. Francis, *Laudato Si'*, para. 201, 131.

88. Francis, *Laudato Si'*, para. 216.

89. Francis, *Laudato Si'*, para. 215.

90. Francis, *Laudato Si'*, para. 215.

91. Francis, *Laudato Si'*, para. 220.

92. Francis, *Laudato Si'*, para. 231.

So, an ecological conversion, a "change of heart"[93] is required, one that prompts us to live out "our vocation to be protectors of God's handiwork."[94]

One of the metaphors which the Pope employs to aid such a "conversion" or "change of heart" toward "God's handiwork"—creation, nature—is that of "home": "We come together to take charge of this *home* which has been entrusted to us."[95] Pope Francis would like us to think of ourselves as related to the rest of life in much the same way as we regard, and relate to, our home. The assumption is that we would take care of the place in which we live, the place to which we so intimately relate.

This is an important point, but it has a significant shortcoming: a number of persons *own* their homes. And with ownership come a sense of possession and a sense of license. Because homes belong to people, they can do with them whatever they like. They are accountable to no one save themselves. While some persons maintain their homes beautifully, some do not.

I have written elsewhere of a slightly different metaphor, one which preserves the point about intimate familiarity and relationship to one's surroundings, but without the sense of ownership and possession.[96] If one were to think of human beings not as owners of the house, but as "house sitters," the negative dimension of possession would be circumvented. For a house sitter does not own the home in which he or she is temporarily living. Instead, the person has been brought in to water the plants, care for the dog or cat, and guarantee the general safety of the house while the true owner is away. The house sitter cannot simply do whatever he or she wants, for the rules of the house have been set by the owner.

In a similar way, the "house" of the creation is owned by God, not by us. God has entrusted the care and protection of the house to us as house sitters, whom he has created and put into the creation to be faithful stewards. We cannot do whatever we want,

93. Australian Catholic Bishops' Conference, "New Earth," 4.

94. Francis, *Laudato Si'*, para. 217.

95. Francis, *Laudato Si'*, para. 244, emphasis mine.

96. E.g., Cain, *Down to Earth*, 55–56.

because God has established rules which are intended to regulate our treatment of God's house. And God expects us house sitters to responsibly live in the house that God has created. The Greek root word for "ecology"—*oikos*—is the same root for the word "house." Ecology involves, in this sense, taking good care of the house— *God's* house—as faithful and responsible house sitters.

Pope Francis concludes his encyclical with a beautiful prayer, several lines of which are applicable here:

> God of love, show us our place in this world
> as channels of your love
> for all the creatures of this earth . . .
> Help us to protect all life.
> AMEN.[97]

Donadio, Rachel. "Cardinals Pick Bergoglio, Who Will Be Pope Francis." *The New York Times,* March 13, 2013. https://www.nytimes.com/2013/03/14/world/europe/cardinals-elect-new-pope.html?pagewanted=all&_r=0.

Gibson, David. "The Story Behind Pope Francis' Election." *USA Today,* March 16, 2013. https://www.usatoday.com/story/news/world/2013/03/16/pope-francis-election-conclave/1992797/.

"Interactive Biography: Pope Francis." *USA Today,* March 3, 2010. http://www.usatoday.com/story/news/world/2013/03/10/cardinal-jorge-mario-bergoglio/1976847/.

Liberia Editrice Vaticana. "Biography of the Holy Father Francis." http://w2.vatican.va/content/francesco/en/biography/documents/papa-francesco-biografia-bergoglio.html.

McElwee, Joshua J. "Cardinals Elect Pope Francis, Argentinean Jesuit Jorge Mario Bergoglio." *National Catholic Reporter,* March 13, 2013. https://www.ncronline.org/news/vatican/cardinals-elect-pope-francis-argentinean-jesuit-jorge-mario-bergoglio.

Pentin, Edward. "Habemus Papum! Pope Francis, a Humble Servant." *National Catholic Register,* March 19, 2013. http://www.ncregister.com/site/article/habemus-papam-pope-francis-a-humble-servant.

"Pope Francis Reveals Why He Chose His Name." *Catholic Herald,* March 16, 2013. http://www.catholicherald.co.uk/news/2013/03/16/pope-francis-reveals-why-he-chose-name.

"Pope Francis's First Encyclical Emphasizes Life-Changing Faith." *United States Conference of Catholic Bishops,* July 5, 2013. http://www.usccb.org/news/2013/13-138e.cfm.

Rocca, Francis X. "Lumen Fidei: An Overview of Pope Francis's First Encyclical." *Catholic Herald,* July 5, 2013. https://catholicherald.co.uk/news/2013/07/05/lumen-fidei-an-overview-of-pope-francis's-first-encyclical/.

Roughneen, Simon. "Pilgrims Hail Pope Francis' Election." *National Catholic Register,* March 19, 2013. http://www.ncregister.com/site/article/pilgrims-hail-pope-francis-election.

Recommendations for Further Reading:

Aguilar, Mario I. *Pope Francis: His Life and Thought*. Cambridge: Lutterworth, 2014.

Brown, Andrew. "The War against Pope Francis." *The Guardian*, October 27, 2017. https://www.theguardian.com/news/2017/oct/27/the-war-against-pope-francis.

Bunson, Matthew E. *Pope Francis*. Huntington: Our Sunday Visitor, 2013.

Francis, Pope. *Care for Creation: A Call for Ecological Conversion*. Edited by Giuliano Vigini. Maryknoll: Orbis, 2016.

———. *Laudato Si': On Care for Our Common Home*. Huntington: Our Sunday Visitor, 2015.

———. *Open Mind, Faithful Heart: Reflections on Following Jesus*. New York: Crossroad, 2012.

Gibson, David. "Five Years of Francis: The Keys to His Papacy." *America: The Jesuit Review*, February 21, 2018. https://www.americamagazine.org/faith/2018/02/21/five-years-francis-keys-his-papacy.

Chapter Five

CONCLUSION

Living in Attunement

IMAGINE LIFE ON THE earth fifty years from now. What will the world be like? Will cancer have been defeated? Will nuclear arms have been dismantled? Will life spans have been elongated to averages of over one hundred years because of breakthroughs in medicine and widespread practices in good health?

And environmentally, what will the world look like? Will we have lost so many species—like the elephant, the tiger, the rhinoceros, the polar bear, and others—that the rich tapestry of life on the planet is threadbare? Or will we have preserved threatened species and retrieved endangered species from the precipice of extinction? Will we have sucked out the last drop of oil to fuel our cars and darkened the skies with our power plants' use of coal? Or will we have turned fully to solar power, wind power, geothermal power, and tidal power as our renewable and perpetual sources of energy?

Will we have stopped the destruction of the rainforest and combatted deforestation by planting record numbers of trees? Or will our planet look bald in photos from interstellar space? Will we have found solutions for our generation of waste? Or will we see garbage strewn around the global community like litter thrown from moving vehicles on major highways? Will we have reversed, or at least arrested, climate change (or, anthropogenic climate disruption, as it has recently been retermed)? Or will the Solomon Islands, the Maldives, Vietnam, Bangladesh, Japan, Ireland, the Netherlands, and coastal areas of the United States like Miami and New York City have become inundated and therefore uninhabitable?

If good, eco-healthy, and sustainable actions will be pursued and the positive scenarios from the list above can be achieved (avoiding the negative ones), then we must change our minds about how we "see" the natural world and, consequently, how we act in it.

Nobel Peace Prize Laureate Wangari Muta Maathai, founder of the Green Belt Movement in Kenya, speaks in her book, *Replenishing the Earth*, of the need for a "shift in perspective" in order to help us deal successfully with the environmental problems that beset planet Earth. She grounds this shift in images and experiences that astronauts have consistently had since the late 1960s, when the first photographs of Earth were sent back from space. These photographs grant a "point-of-viewing" which dramatically shows the earth as a "beautiful blue orb seemingly suspended in an endless darkness."[1] She then selects the comments of several international astronauts whose ways of "seeing" were dramatically changed and lives were irreversibly transformed from witnessing the earth from that vantage point. James Irwin, the eighth person to walk on the moon, was struck by the fragility and delicateness of the "beautiful, warm, living planet" he saw hanging in space. Seeing this changed him and helped him "appreciate the creation of God and the love of God," and he later became a minister.[2] The sixth man on the moon, Edgar Mitchell, said that when he viewed our planet, he had a "glimpse of divinity" and returned converted as a "humanitarian."[3] The Bulgarian cosmonaut Aleksandr Alek-

1. Maathai, *Replenishing the Earth*, 59.
2. Maathai, *Replenishing the Earth*, 60.
3. Maathai, *Replenishing the Earth*, 60.

sandrov gained the insight that all of us humans are "Earth's children," and that we should treat the earth "as our Mother."[4]

Commander Eileen Collins, aboard the *Discovery* in a mission almost fifteen years ago, remembers also seeing fires burning in central Africa, due to slash-and-burn agriculture being practiced and charcoal being produced. She wondered: How could persons not take better care of the earth and replace the resources that had been used? If they could just see things from the perspective of astronauts, she thought, they would behave in quite different ways.[5]

If they could just see things from another perspective!

At this present moment in time, we face environmental challenges of unprecedented proportions: deforestation is occurring at an alarming rate; species extinction is proceeding with unprecedented speed, a pace not experienced by the earth's ecosystems since the demise of the dinosaurs[6]; water pollution continues unabated, while desertification claims more and more fertile land and turns it into sand; we are running out of oil, and coal (though much more plentiful) is an extremely dirty fuel to burn; overfishing has reduced ocean species to dangerous levels and depleted some entirely; human overpopulation is accelerating exponentially as we add one billion persons to the world about every decade—at this rate, even generous calculations of carrying capacity ("K," the number of people the earth's resources and environmental systems can successfully accommodate) will be exceeded. Climate change threatens not only the stability of the planet but also the survival of life upon it. Garbage is headed to landfills (each of which is filling up and we are running out of additional locations), to ocean dumping sites (where natural equilibria are jeopardized), and to incinerators (which, unless filtered, fill the air with toxins; and we must still dispose of the ash residue that remains). Fresh water is becoming in shorter and shorter supply, and this environmental

4. Maathai, *Replenishing the Earth*, 60.
5. Maathai, *Replenishing Earth*, 57.
6. Kolbert, *Sixth Extinction*.

insecurity creates tensions and raises anxieties for violence and war.

These conditions are due to human action, to behaviors that result from a way of looking at things. In this way of looking, our actions are outward, noticeable symptoms of an underlying, internal disease—an unhealthy way of looking at the natural world. Our proclivity is to see nature as a vast storehouse of objects, of goods, of products, there for our taking. Their only value lies in our satisfaction. And we are apparently never satisfied—our greed for these goods knows no end. We *Homo sapiens* have a tendency to picture ourselves at the top of the heap and regard nonhuman living entities as objects, as "things," which reside below us. We dominate. We tame. We conquer. We bend nature to our will. And sometimes we turn to the Bible to sanction our domination or to get our marching orders in the first place ("have dominion" and "subdue"—Gen 1:26–28). Didn't God give us a mandate to have this dominion and to do this subduing? Are we not in charge of earth and its resources? Our perspective determines our treatment.

If nature had a human voice, it would shout, "Ouch! Enough! That hurts!" If creation had the demonstrative power to protest, it would resist and exclaim, "Stop it! Don't you see that this is unfair? Can't you see you are harming yourselves and jeopardizing your survival when you harm nature and violate its integrity?" And yet, what we see happening on our earth and to our planet gives us a warning. The warning bells and lights are going off; the canary in the coal mine has stopped singing. But we are not listening to nature's message. We are not attuned to creation's cries.

Science can raise our consciousness. The scientific data can grab our attention. The natural sciences can make us aware of what's going on and of the threats that indict the foolishness of our actions and that imperil our survival. In fact, for decades now, scientists have been trying to inform us and to appeal to our good-will, if not our self-interest.

And religion can prick our consciences. Religion can remind us that we were created to take good care of and protect the planet (Gen 2:15), the creation which God has so trustingly placed in our hands. Religion can spur us to action. For religion does not have to be part of the problem, seeming to justify the exploitation, abuse, and misuse; religion can be part of the solution.

Bottom line, we must change our perspective:

> From one of dominance to one of care-giving;
>
> From one of being served, to one of providing service;
>
> From one of we are apart from nature, to one of we are a part of nature;
>
> From one of we are at the vertical top and we lord it over,
>
> to one of we are strands in the horizontal web and we work with;
>
> From one of power over, to one of solidarity with;
>
> From one of seeing nature as a commodity to be used,
>
> to one of seeing nature as a community in which to live and with which to relate;
>
> From one of pride, to one of humility;
>
> From one of indifference, to one of compassion;
>
> From one of disrespect, to one of honor;
>
> From one of disharmony, to one of harmony;
>
> From one of desecration, to one of reverence;
>
> From one of autism, to one of attunement.

Religion can assist, must assist, with this change of perspective. The religions of the world have the resources to equip this transformation from one unsustainable way of seeing to another sustainable way of seeing. For with this change in perspective can come, will come, a change in action. As a matter of fact, how we "see" will influence at the very least, and determine at the very most, how we will "act." This change, this transformation, involves repentance (a change of direction, a turning around) and *metanoia* (a change of heart).

From our four historical figures, we have gained both insight and inspiration for this alteration of perspective, this turning around, this change of heart. Each person stood within his/her time, but also stood out from that time. Hildegard was a woman of her time, and as we have seen was in some ways traditional, but in many other ways innovative and even revolutionary. Recall her tapping of plants and minerals as cures for diseases and ailments—a prolepsis of the future when such a large number of our drugs are taken from the herbal bounty of the rainforest. She also reminded us that God is present in the creation and that makes nature holy and sacred. And she proposed *viriditas* as the greening and unifying principle present and at work in everything that exists.

Francis was brought up in a time of economic prosperity as a member of a wealthy family. His dream of becoming a knight and of pledging allegiance to his lady in courtly love was transformed into his becoming a monk and pledging loyalty to Lady Poverty. His view of nature as good (because a good God had created it), as consisting of creatures who were subjects with intrinsic worth who deserved our reverence, and as all related to one another and to human beings as siblings in the human family headed by a Creator God was revolutionary. His "Canticle to the Creatures"—Brother Sun and Sister Moon—encapsulates much of what he emphasized.

Ryōkan was an idiosyncratic and eccentric monk who lived a life of humility and simplicity. Eschewing any privileged position save a tattered robe and a begging bowl, he lived in a rustic hut and ate food obtained through the generosity of others. He appreciated the beauty of nature, and the poems he wrote reveal his deep love for the natural world and his denial of material things as a means and guarantor of happiness.

Pope Francis wears the impressive symbols of his office and is the instantly recognized leader of over one billion Roman Catholics worldwide. But his humility and identification with the poor—coupled with his application of religious resources for addressing ecological problems and his affirmation of climate change and human culpability for it—are at odds with the traditional power and perks of his position and in many ways unprecedented for the papacy. He challenges us to take better care of "our common home."

Nature speaks to us. And these four voices speak to us. But we must have the willingness and ability to hear them. We must not turn a deaf ear. We must live in attunement.

BIBLIOGRAPHY

Abé, Ryūichi. "Poetics of Mendicancy." In *Great Fool: Zen Master Ryōkan*, edited by Ryūichi Abé and Peter Haskel, Honolulu: University of Hawai'i Press, 1996.

Abé, Ryūichi, and Peter Haskel. *Great Fool: Zen Master Ryōkan*. Honolulu: University of Hawai'i Press, 1996.

Aguilar, Mario I. *Pope Francis: His Life and Thought*. Cambridge: Lutterworth, 2014.

Allen, John L., Jr. *The Miracle of Francis*. New York: Time, 2015.

"Amazon Rainforest Facts." www.medicinehunter.com/amazon-rainforest-facts/.

Apse, Will. "Medieval Women: Love, Marriage, Family, and Livelihoods." https://owlcation.com/humanities/medieval-women.

Araies, Philippe, and Georges Duby, eds. *Revelations of the Medieval World*. Vol. 2 of *A History of Private Life*. Cambridge: Harvard University Press, 1988.

Armstrong, Edward A. *Saint Francis: Nature Mystic*. Berkeley: University of California Press, 1973.

Armstrong, Regis, et al., eds. *Francis of Assisi: Early Documents*. The Assisi Compilation. 3 vols. Hyde Park: New City, 1999–2001.

Australian Catholic Bishops' Conference. "A New Earth: The Environmental Challenge." https://www.socialjustice.catholic.org.au/files/SJSandresources/2002_SJSS_statement.pdf.

Baird, Joseph L., and Radd K. Ehrman, eds. *The Letters of Hildegard of Bingen*. 3 vols. Oxford: Oxford University Press, 1994, 1998, 2004.

Benedict, Pope, XVI. "Address of His Holiness Benedict XVI to Students Participating in a Meeting Promoted by the 'Sister Nature' Foundation." https://w2.vatican.va/content/benedict-xvi/en/speeches/2011/november/documents/hf_ben-xvi_spe_20111128_sorella-natura.html.

———. "Visit to the Federal Parliament in the Reichstag Building." https://www.ewtn.com/catholicism/library/visit-to-the-federal-parliament-in-the-reichstag-building-12871.

Berry, Thomas. *The Dream of the Earth*. San Francisco: Sierra Club, 1988.

———. *The Great Work: Our Way into the Future*. New York: Bell Tower, 1999.

Berry, Wendell. "Christianity and Survival of Creation." *Crosscurrents* 43 (Summer 1993) 149–64.

Bishop, Jane. "Co-Translator's Note." In *Hildegard of Bingen: Scivias*, translated by Mother Columba Hart and Jane Bishop, 56. Mahwah: Paulist, 1990.

Blockmans, Wim. "Urbanization in the European Middle Ages." In *Living in the City: Urban Institutions in the Low Countries, 1200–2010*, by Leo Lucassen and Wim Willems, 1–11. New York: Routledge, 2011.

Boff, Leonardo. *The Prayer of St. Francis*. Maryknoll: Orbis, 2001.

———. *Saint Francis: A Model for Human Liberation*. New York: Crossroad, 1982.

Bosker, Martin. "The Development of Cities in Italy." *Working Paper* 1893 (January 2007) 1–43.

Bovey, Alixe. "Women in Medieval Society." *The Middle Ages* (blog), April 30, 2015. http://www.bl.uk/the-middle-ages/articles/women-in-medieval-society.

Bowie, Fiona, and Oliver Davies, eds. *Hildegard of Bingen: Mystical Writings*. Translated by Robert Carver. London: SPCK, 1996.

Bowler, Kate. *Blessed: A History of the American Prosperity Gospel*. Oxford: Oxford University Press, 2013.

———. "Death, the Prosperity Gospel and Me." *The New York Times*, February 13, 2016. https://www.nytimes.com/2016/02/14/opinion/sunday/death-the-prosperity-gospel-and-me.html.

Bronforte, Ugolino. *The Little Flowers of St. Francis*. Mineola, NY: Dover, 2003.

Brother Leo. *The Mirror of Perfection*. Larger version. Edited by Paul Sabatier. Translated by Sebastian Evans. London: Nutt, 1900.

Brown, Andrew. "The War against Pope Francis." *The Guardian*, October 27, 2017. https://www.theguardian.com/news/2017/oct/27/the-war-against-pope-francis.

Brueggemann, Walter. *The God of All Flesh and Other Essays*. Edited by K. C. Hanson. Cambridge: Clarke, 2015.

Buber, Martin. *I and Thou*. Mansfield Centre, CT: Martino, 2010.

Bunson, Matthew E. *Pope Francis*. Huntington: Our Sunday Visitor, 2013.

Caesarius. *Rule for Nuns of St. Caesarius of Arles*. Translated by M. C. McCarthy. Studies in Mediaeval History 16. Washington, DC: Catholic Society of America, 1960.

Cain, Clifford Chalmers. *Down to Earth: Religious Paths toward Custodianship of Nature*. Lanham: University Press of America, 2009.

———. *Many Heavens, One Earth*. Lanham: Lexington, 2012.

———. "Self-Reliant and Ecologically Aware: A Christian Appreciation of Buddhism." In *Learning from Other Religious Traditions: Leaving Room for Holy Envy,* edited by Hans Gustafson, 117–35. Cham, Switzerland: Macmillan, 2018.

Canadian Conference of Catholic Bishops. "You Love All that Exists . . . All Things are Yours, God, Lover of Life." http://www.cccb.ca/site/Files/pastoralenvironment.html.

Carson, Rachel. *Silent Spring.* Greenwich: Fawcett, 1962.

Catechism of the Catholic Church. http://www.vatican.va/archive/ccc_css/archive/catechism/p1s2c1p4.htm.

Chesterton, G. K. *St. Francis of Assisi.* New York: Doubleday, 1990.

Chowaney, Nonin. "Ryokan." http://www.chzc.org/Nonin2.htm.

Chryssavgis, John. *On Earth as in Heaven: Ecological Vision and Initiatives of Ecumenical Patriarch Bartholomew.* Bronx: Fordham University Press, 2012.

Cook, William R., and Ronald B. Herzman. *The Medieval Worldview.* New York: Oxford University Press, 2001.

Cool, Michael. *Francis: A New World Pope.* Grand Rapids: Eerdmans, 2013.

Cron, Ian Morgan. *Chasing Francis: A Pilgrim's Tale.* Grand Rapids: Zondervan, 2013.

Cullmann, Oscar. *Immortality of the Soul or Resurrection of the Dead?* London: Epworth, 1964.

Delio, Ilia, et al. *Care for Creation: A Franciscan Spirituality of the Earth.* Cincinnati: St. Anthony Messenger, 2008.

D'Evelyn, Stephen. Review of *The Letters of Hildegard of Bingen, Vol. III,* edited by Joseph L. Baird and Radd K. Ehrman. *Bryn Mawr Classical Review* 6.6 (2004).

Dominican Episcopal Conference. "Pastoral Letter on the Relationship of Human Beings to Nature." http://www.inee.mu.edu/documents/18DominicanEpiscopalConference_000.pdf.

Donadio, Rachel. "Cardinals Pick Bergoglio, Who Will Be Pope Francis." *The New York Times,* March 13, 2013. https://www.nytimes.com/2013/03/14/world/europe/cardinals-elect-new-pope.html?pagewanted=all&_r=0.

Doyle, Eric. *Saint Francis and the Song of the Brotherhood.* London: Allen & Unwin, 1980.

Dronke, Peter. *Women Writers of the Middle Ages.* Cambridge: Cambridge University Press, 1996.

Duby, Georges. *Eleanor of Aquitaine and Six Others.* Vol. 1 of *Women of the Twelfth Century.* Oxford: Polity, 1997.

———. *Eve and the Church.* Vol. 3 of *Women of the Twelfth Century.* Oxford: Polity, 1998.

———. *Remembering the Dead.* Vol. 2 of *Women of the Twelfth Century.* Oxford: Polity, 1997.

Duehren, Caitlyn. "From the Mouth of God: Hildegard of Bingen's Biblical Hermeneutics." *Journal of Theta Alpha Kappa* 35 (Spring 2011) 83.

Flanagan, Sabina. *Hildegard of Bingen: A Visionary Life.* New York: Routledge, 1998.

Fox, Matthew. *Illuminations of Hildegard of Bingen*. Rochester, VT: Bear, 2002.

Francis, Pope. *Care for Creation: A Call for Ecological Conversion*. Edited by Giuliano Vigini. Maryknoll: Orbis, 2016.

———. *Laudato Si': On Care for Our Common Home*. Huntington: Our Sunday Visitor, 2015.

———. "Meeting with Young People." http://w2.vatican.va/content/francesco/en/speeches/2015/january/documents/papa-francesco_20150118_srilanka-filippine-incontro-giovani.html.

———. *Open Mind, Faithful Heart: Reflections on Following Jesus*. New York: Crossroad, 2012.

Guardini, Romano. *The End of the Modern World*. Wilmington, DE: ISI Books, 2001.

Gautier, Léon. *La Chevalerie*. Paris: Delagrave, 1891.

Gibson, David. "The Story Behind Pope Francis' Election." *USA Today*, March 16, 2013. https://www.usatoday.com/story/news/world/2013/03/16/pope-francis-election-conclave/1992797/.

Godefridus of Disibodenberg, and Theodoric of Echternach. *Vita Sanctae Hildegardis* [*The Life of the Saintly Hildegard*]. Translated and edited by Hugh Feiss. Toronto: Peregrina, 1996.

Gore, Al. *Earth in Balance: Ecology and the Human Spirit*. New York: Houghton Mifflin, 1992.

Greenway, William. *Agape Ethics: Moral Realism and Love for All Life*. Eugene, OR: Cascade, 2016.

———. *For the Love of All Creatures*. Grand Rapids: Eerdmans, 2015.

Habig, Marion A., ed. *Saint Francis of Assisi: Omnibus of Sources, vol. 1*. Quincy, IL: Franciscan Press, 1991.

———. *St. Francis of Assisi: Writings and Early Biographies*. Translated by Benen Fahy. Chicago: Franciscan Herald, 1973.

Hall, Douglas John. *Imaging God: Dominion as Stewardship*. Chester Heights, PA: Friendship, 1986.

Hendry, George. *Theology of Nature*. Philadelphia: Westminster, 1980.

Hildegard of Bingen. *Causae et Curae* [*Causes and Cures*]. Translated by Priscilla Throop. Charlotte, VT: MedievalMS, 2012.\

———. *Hildegard of Bingen: Scivias*. Translated by Mother Columba Hart and Jane Bishop. Mahwah: Paulist, 1990.

———. *Liber Divinorum Operum*. Edited by Albert Derolez and Peter Fronke. Corpus Christianorum Continuatio Mediaevalis 92. Turnholti: Brepols, 1996.

House, Adrian. *Francis of Assisi: A Revolutionary Life*. Mahwah: Paulist, 2001.

Hughes, Johnson Donald. *American Indian Ecology*. Ann Arbor: University of Michigan Press, 1983.

"In Memoriam." http://www.rachelcarson.org/mRachelCarson.aspx.

"Interactive Biography: Pope Francis." *USA Today*, March 3, 2010. http://www.usatoday.com/story/news/world/2013/03/10/cardinal-jorge-mario-bergoglio/1976847/.

Jeffers, Susan. *Brother Eagle, Sister Sky*. New York: Dial, 1991.

"John Muir: 'I Asked the Boulders Where They Had Been.'" *Infospigot: The Chronicles* (blog), September 29, 2009. https://infospigot.typepad.com/ infospigot_the_chronicles/2009/09/john-muir-i-asked-the-boulders-where-they-had-been.html.

John Paul, Pope, II. *Catechesis*. August 2, 2000. https://w2.vatican.va/content/ john-paul-ii/en/audiences/2000/documents/hf_jp-ii_aud_20000802. html.

———. *Catechesis*. January 17, 2001. https://w2.vatican.va/content/john-paul-ii/en/audiences/2001/documents/hf_jp-ii_aud_20010117.html.

———. *Message for the 1990 World Day of Peace*. January 1, 1990. http:// w2.vatican.va/content/john-paul-ii/en/messages/peace/documents/hf_ jp-ii_mes_19891208_xxiii-world-day-for-peace.html.

———. *Redemptor Hominis*. http://w2.vatican.va/content/john-paul-ii/en/ encyclicals/documents/hf_jp-ii_enc_04031979_redemptor-hominis. html.

Keller, Evelyn Fox. *A Feeling for the Organism: The Life and Work of Barbara McClintock*. New York: Holt, 1983.

Kettle, Ann. Review of *Women of the Twelfth Century*, by George Duby. *Reviews in History* 73 (June 1999). https://archives.history.ac.uk/history-in-focus/ Gender/kettle.html.

King-Lenzmeier, Anne H. *Hildegard of Bingen: An Integrated Vision*. Collegeville: Liturgical, 2001.

Kirkpatrick, David Paul. "Paul Tillich on Nature: 'Nature Is Not Only Glorious; It Is Also Tragic.'" *David Paul Kirkpatrick's Living in the Metaverse* (blog), October 29, 2012. https://www.davidpaulkirkpatrick.com/2012/10/29/ paul-tillich-on-nature-nature-is-not-only-glorious-it-is-also-tragic/.

Kolbert, Elizabeth. *The Sixth Extinction: An Unnatural History*. New York: Holt, 2014.

Kownachi, Mary Lou. *Between Two Souls: Conversations with Ryōkan*. Grand Rapids: Eerdmans, 2004.

Krech, Shepherd, III. *The Ecological Indians*. New York: Norton, 2000.

Liberia Editrice Vaticana. "Biography of the Holy Father Francis." http:// w2.vatican.va/content/francesco/en/biography/documents/papa-francesco-biografia-bergoglio.html.

Linzey, Andrew. *Animal Gospel*. Louisville: Westminster John Knox, 1999.

———. *Animal Theology*. Champaign: University of Illinois Press, 1995.

———. *Christianity and the Rights of Animals*. New York: Crossroad, 1987.

———. *Why Animal Suffering Matters*. Oxford: Oxford University Press, 2013.

Maathai, Wangari. *Replenishing the Earth: Spiritual Values for Healing Ourselves and the Earth*. New York: Doubleday, 2010.

Maddocks, Fiona. *Hildegard of Bingen: The Woman of Her Age*. New York: Doubleday, 2001.

Madigan, Shawn. *Mystics, Visionaries, and Prophets*. Minneapolis: Fortress, 1998.

Martin, Valerie. *Salvation Scenes from the Life of St. Francis.* New York: Vintage, 2001.

McDaniel, Jay B. *Good News for Animals: Christian Appreciation for Animal Well-Being.* Eugene, OR: Wipf & Stock, 1993.

———. "Living From the Center." https://www.spiritualityandpractice.com/book-reviews/excerpts/view/13563/living-from-the-center.

———. *Of God and Pelicans: A Theology of Reverence for Life.* Louisville: Westminster John Knox, 1989.

McElwee, Joshua J. "Cardinals Elect Pope Francis, Argentinean Jesuit Jorge Mario Bergoglio." *National Catholic Reporter*, March 13, 2013. https://www.ncronline.org/news/vatican/cardinals-elect-pope-francis-argentinean-jesuit-jorge-mario-bergoglio.

McFague, Sallie. *The Body of God: An Ecological Theology.* Minneapolis: Fortress, 1993.

———. "The World as God's Body." *The Christian Century*, July 20–27, 1998.

McKibben, Bill. *The End of Nature.* New York: Random House, 2006.

Meng-hu. "Zen Poetics of Ryokan." *Simply Haiku: A Quarterly Journal of Japanese Short Form Poetry* 4.2 (Summer 2006). http://www.simplyhaiku.com/SHv4n2/features/Meng-hu.html.

Merchant, Carolyn. *The Death of Nature.* New York: Harper & Row, 1980.

———. "Environmentalism: From the Control of Nature to Partnership." https://nature.berkeley.edu/departments/espm/env-hist/Moses.pdf.

Mews, Constant. "Religious Thinker." In *Voice of the Living Light: Hildegard of Bingen and Her World,* edited by Barbara Newman, 52–69. Berkeley: University of California Press, 1998.

Migne, J. P. "Saint Hildegard of Bingen and the *Vita S. Hildegardis.*" *Tjurunga: An Australasian Benedictine Review* 29 (1985) 4–25; 30 (1986) 63–73; 31 (1986) 32–41; 32 (1987) 46–59.

Mitchell, Stephen, ed. *The Enlightened Heart: An Anthology of Sacred Poetry.* New York: HarperCollins, 1989.

Nasr, Syeed Hossein. "Religion and the Resacralization of Nature." In *Religion and the Order of Nature,* 270–92. Oxford: Oxford University Press, 1996.

Neihardt, John G. *Black Elk Speaks.* Lincoln, NE: University of Nebraska Press, 1985.

New Catholic Encyclopedia. 15 vols. 2nd ed. Farmington Hills, MI: Cengage Gale, 2002.

Newman, Barbara J. "Hildegard of Bingen: Visions and Validation." *Church History* 54 (1985) 163–75.

———. "Introduction." In *Hildegard of Bingen: Scivias,* translated by Mother Columba Hart and Jane Bishop, 9–54. Mahwah: Paulist, 1990.

———. *Sister of Wisdom: St. Hildegard's Theology of the Feminine.* Berkeley: University of California Press, 1987.

Newman, Barbara J., ed. *Hildegard of Bingen: Scivias.* Translated by Mother Columba Hart and Jane Bishop. Mahwah: Paulist, 1990.

———. *Voice of the Living Light: Hildegard of Bingen and Her World*. Berkeley: University of California Press, 1998.

Newport, Frank. "2017 Update on Americans and Religion." *Gallup*, December 22, 2017. https://news.gallup.com/poll/224642/2017-update-americans-religion.aspx.

———. *God Is Alive and Well: The Future of Religion in America*. New York: Gallup, 2012.

Nothwehr, Dawn M. *Ecological Footprints: An Essential Franciscan Guide for Faith and Sustainable Living*. Collegeville: Liturgical, 2012.

"Owed to Nature: Medicines from Tropic Forests." https://www.rainforesttrust.org/owed-to-nature-medicines-from-tropical-forests/.

Pan-chui Lai. "Paul Tillich and Ecological Theology." *The Journal of Religion* 79 (April 1999) 233–49.

Patriarch Bartholomew. "Address of Ecumenical Patriarch Bartholomew at the Environmental Symposium, Saint Barbara Greek Orthodox Church, Santa Barbara, California." https://www.apostolicpilgrimage.org/the-environment/-/asset_publisher/4hInlautXpQ3/content/address-of-ecumenical-patriarch-bartholomew-at-the-environmental-symposium-saint-barbara-greek-orthodox-church-santa-barbara-california/32008?inheritRedirect=false--------------It.

———. "Visit of Pope Paul VI: To the FAO on the 25th Anniversary of Its Institution." https://w2.vatican.va/content/paul-vi/en/speeches/1970/documents/hf_p-vi_spe_19701116_xxv-istituzione-fao.html.

Paul, Pope, VI. *Octogesima Adveniens*. http://w2.vatican.va/content/paul-vi/en/apost_letters/documents/hf_p-vi_apl_19710514_octogesima-adveniens.html.

Pentin, Edward. "Habemus Papum! Pope Francis, a Humble Servant." *National Catholic Register*, March 19, 2013. http://www.ncregister.com/site/article/habemus-papam-pope-francis-a-humble-servant.

"Pope Francis Biography." https://www.biography.com/religious-figure/pope-francis.

"Pope Francis Reveals Why He Chose His Name." *Catholic Herald*, March 16, 2013. http://www.catholicherald.co.uk/news/2013/03/16/pope-francis-reveals-why-he-chose-name.

"Pope Francis's First Encyclical Emphasizes Life-Changing Faith." *United States Conference of Catholic Bishops*, July 5, 2013. http://www.usccb.org/news/2013/13-138e.cfm.

Power, Eileen. *Medieval Women*. Cambridge: Cambridge University Press, 1995.

Quinn, Daniel. *Ishmael*. New York: Bantam, 1992.

Radice, Betty. *The Letters of Abelard and Heloise*. New York: Penguin Classics, 2003.

Rocca, Francis X. "Lumen Fidei: An Overview of Pope Francis's First Encyclical." *Catholic Herald*, July 5, 2013. https://catholicherald.co.uk/

news/2013/07/05/lumen-fidei-an-overview-of-pope-francis's-first-encyclical/.

Rosenwein, Barbara. *A Short History of the Middle Ages.* New York: Broadview, 2004.

Ross, David. *1,001 Pearls of Wisdom.* San Francisco: Chronicle, 2006.

Roth, Stephanie. "The Cosmic Vision of Hildegard of Bingen." *The Ecologist* 30.1 (2000) 40–42.

Roughneen, Simon. "Pilgrims Hail Pope Francis' Election." *National Catholic Register,* March 19, 2013. http://www.ncregister.com/site/article/pilgrims-hail-pope-francis-election.

Ruether, Rosemary Radford. *Visionary Women: Three Medieval Mystics.* Minneapolis: Fortress, 2002.

Ryall, Julian. "Woman Arborist Heals Trees, Parks, and Souls." *Nippon.com,* May 9, 2016. https://www.nippon.com/en/people/e00096/woman-arborist-heals-trees-parks-souls.html.

Sacks, Oliver. *Migraine: Understanding a Common Disorder.* Berkeley: University of California Press, 1985.

Saint Bonaventure. *The Life of St. Francis.* Mahwah: Paulist, 1978.

———. *Major Life of Francis.* Translated by Ewert Cousins. New York: HarperCollins, 2005.

"Saint Francis & the Wolf." http://tamingthewolf.com/saint-francis-and-the-wolf/.

Saint Francis of Assisi. "Canticle of the Creatures." In *Francis of Assisi, Early Documents, Vol. I: The Saint,* edited by Regis J. Armstrong, 113. Hyde Park: New City, 1999.

Sagan, Carl. *Cosmos.* New York: Random House, 1980.

Schipperges, Heinrich. *Hildegard von Bingen: Healing and the Nature of the Cosmos.* Munich: Beck, 1995.

Schweitzer, Albert. "The Ethics of Reverence for Life." *Christendom* 1 (Winter 1936) 125–39.

———. *Out of My Life and Thought.* New York: Holt, Rinehart & Winston, 1949.

———. *The Philosophy of Civilization.* New York: Macmillan, 1949.

———. *The Teaching of Reverence for Life.* New York: Holt, Rinehart & Winston, 1965.

Share, Mary Elizabeth. "The Spirituality and Mysticism of Nature in the Early Franciscan Tradition." PhD diss., University of South Africa, 2004.

Sheth, Sonam, et al. "7 Charts that Show the Glaring Gap between Men and Women's Salaries in the US." *Business Insider,* August 23, 2019. https://www.businessinsider.com/gender-wage-pay-gap-charts-2017-3.

Singer, Charles, ed. "The Scientific Views and Visions of Saint Hildegard." In *Studies in the History and Method of Science,* 1:1–55. 2 vols. Oxford: Clarendon, 1917.

Sorrell, Roger. *St. Francis of Assisi and Nature.* New York: Oxford University Press, 1988.

Stevens, John. *Dewdrops on a Lotus Leaf: Zen Poems of Ryōkan*. Boston: Shambhala, 1993.

—————. *One Robe, One Bowl: The Zen Poetry of Ryōkan*. Boston: Weatherhill, 2014.

—————. *Three Zen Masters: Ikkyū, Hakuin, and Ryōkan*. Tokyo: Kodansha, 1993.

Tanahashi, Kazuaki. *Sky Above, Great Wind: The Life and Poetry of Zen Master Ryokan*. Boulder: Shambhala, 2012.

Taylor, Barbara Brown. *An Altar in the World: A Geography of Faith*. New York: HarperCollins, 2009.

Theokritoff, Elizabeth. "From Sacramental Life to Sacramental Living." *Greek Orthodox Theological Review* 44 (1990) 505–24.

—————. "The Orthodox Church and the Environmental Movement." In *Many Heavens, One Earth: Readings on Religion and the Environment*, edited by Clifford Chalmers Cain, 63–79. Lanham: Lexington, 2012.

Thomas of Celano. *First Life of St. Francis of Assisi*. London: SPCK, 2000.

—————. *The Francis Trilogy*. Hyde Park: New City, 2004.

—————. *The Lives of St. Francis of Assisi*. London: Methuen, 1908.

Thompson, Augustine. "Hildegard of Bingen on Gender and the Priesthood." *Church History* 6.3 (September 1994) 349–84.

Tillich, Paul. *Dynamics of Faith*. New York: Harper & Row, 1957.

—————. *Reason and Revelation, Being and God*. Vol. 1 of *Systematic Theology*. Chicago: University of Chicago Press, 1951.

Toynbee, Arnold. "The Religious Background of the Environmental Crisis." *The International Journal of Environmental Studies* 3 (1972) 141–46.

Trueman, C. N. "Medieval Women." https://www.historylearningsite.co.uk/medieval-england/medieval-women/.

Uhlein, Gabriele. *Meditations with Hildegard of Bingen*. Santa Fe: Bear, 1982.

Vian, Nello, ed. *The Sayings of Brother Giles*. St. Bonaventure: Franciscan Institute, 1990.

von Trotta, Margarethe, dir. *Vision: From the Life of Hildegard von Bingen*. 2009; New York: Zeitgeist Films.

Warner, Keith. "St. Francis: Patron Saint of Ecology." *U.S. Catholic Reporter* 75 (April 2010) 25.

Watson, Burton. *Ryōkan: Zen Monk, Poet of Japan*. New York: Columbia University Press, 1977.

White, Lynn, Jr. "The Historical Roots of Our Ecologic Crisis." *Science* 155 (March 10, 1967) 1203–7.

Wilson, E. O. *Biophilia*. Cambridge: Harvard University Press, 1984.

Yuasa, Nobuyuki. *The Zen Poems of Ryōkan*. Princeton: Princeton University Press, 1981.

Yuasa, Nobuyuki, trans. "You Do Not Need Many Things." http://www.poetseers.org/spiritual-and-devotional-poets/buddhist/ryokan/ryokanp/you-do-not-need/

INDEX

Index